The Clouded C
JAMES NAYLEF

CW01475743

To A.S.M.
a relentless pursuer
of completion,
now able to relax with me

James Nayler riding into Bristol in 1656, by Robert Spence. Courtesy of Friends House Library.

The Clouded Quaker Star
JAMES NAYLER
1618 to 1660

by
Vera Massey

Sessions Book Trust, York, England
in association with
Friends United Press, Richmond, Indiana, USA

UK   ISBN 1 85072 224 2

USA ISBN 0 944350 46 1

Library of Congress Cataloging-in-Publication Data
Massey, Vera.
    The Clouded Quaker Star: James Nayler, 1618-1660 / by Vera Massey.
    p. cm.
    Includes bibliographical references and index.
    ISBN 1-85072-224-2 (UK) -- ISBN 0-944350-46-1 (US)
    1. Naylor, James, 1617?-1660. 2. Quakers--England --Biography. I. Title.
BX7795.N39.M37 1999
289.6'092--dc21
[B]   99-042797

The sketches on pages vi, 8, 17, 50, 59, 68 and 89
are by David Barlow, newly drawn
for this publication.

Printed in 11 on 12 point Plantin Typeface
by Sessions of York
The Ebor Press
York, England

Contents

Chapter		Page
I	'Of Yeoman Stock'	1
II	Confronting the Light	9
III	Swarthmoor	18
IV	To London	28
V	Martha	41
VI	A Sign	51
VII	Bristol	60
VIII	Purgatory	69
IX	Restoration	81
X	Power above Pride	90
XI	Postscript: The Seeds of Time	103
	Index	110

Illustrations

James Nayler riding into Bristol in 1656, by Robert Spence. Courtesy of Friends House Library ... ...*Frontispiece*

James, seated in Exeter prison, with visiting George Fox, by David Barlow vi

James preaching to the people, by David Barlow 8

James looking at his sleeping children, by David Barlow ... 17

James Lancaster's wife stoning George Fox, by Robert Spence. Courtesy of Friends House Library ... 27

Title Page of 'A Lamentacion' and of 'A Warning' 40

Martha Simmonds with James Nayler, by David Barlow ... 50

'Dorcas arise', by David Barlow 59

Robert Rich, by David Barlow 68

General John Lambert 80

Anne Nayler drafting her petition, by David Barlow 89

James Nayler, reproduced from *Klachte der Quakers* 109

James Nayler, seated in Exeter prison, offers visiting George Fox an apple:
'This fateful moment' see page 56.

CHAPTER I

'Of Yeoman Stock'

THE WORLD, AS A concept seen through the eyes of an English farming family in 1618, was pretty remote. It was especially irrelevant to people's lives in the West Riding of Yorkshire, where most workers were unlikely to have even seen the sea. Their work was their life, and the dominant theme was agriculture, including care of the sheep that scattered the high moorlands adjoining the great Plain of York. Any news that reached them probably came from the parson or the carriers and pedlars of any necessaries they could not provide themselves.

Somewhere beyond the horizon lay the imperishable cities planted by the Romans – London, Bristol, Lincoln, Chester, York – whose plans and boundaries had not altered much in a thousand years. The tail end of the Virgin Queen's blaze of glory was said to be still a-sparkle in court masques devised by Ben Jonson and decorated by Inigo Jones, but the patronage of a stage-struck Danish Queen and the cumbersome presence of a sexually ambivalent Scottish monarch were no substitute for departed splendours. Court masques were the Queen's or the universities' playthings, and could not travel as the old histories and romances had done, to reach the people in times of plague or summer recess. Shakespeare had taken early retirement after his token gesture towards the masque-form in *The Tempest*, and had died in the odour of gentility two years earlier.

For the English people, as the Stuarts settled in, a new restlessness was beginning to be felt. A major revelation was the translation of the Bible into common speech, which made religion no longer the prerogative of the study and the parsonage. Conquests and semi-respectable piracy had emphasised national pride without taking it much beyond the borders of England itself; 'Great Britain' was an undiscovered ordering in the mind of James I. Turbulence prevailed in Scotland and Ireland, but in the West Riding villages church and manorial rights were the vital issues.

Over the course of history down to the present day Yorkshire has been a remaining refuge of those who long for space and independence. It has a lingering sense of a moon-like landscape now only surviving in the dales and moors, but to be felt even around the smaller towns in the seventeenth century. This was the setting in the 1620's for the childhood of James Nayler. His biographers have acknowledged a strange silence, even a mystery, to have fallen over his early years. In the absence of friendly records facts can be gathered mainly from his opponents, never a complimentary source. In describing his father as a 'sow-gelder' a hostile pamphleteer was probably selecting one of the less presentable jobs of his daily round as a farmer.

Certainly the house that was sketched in 1843 as Nayler's reputed 'residence' (whether as juvenile or later) was no labourer's cottage. Ardsley Hall, two miles from Wakefield, appears to have been built on an Elizabethan E-plan, with Cotswold-style square dripstones over mullioned windows, wide gables and a central entrance. The debate over the Nayler family's exact social standing seems never to have been settled. James described himself as a 'husbandman', meaning literally one who has a household. The term 'yeoman' itself has had various interpretations. Probably it signifies a forerunner of what would later be called lower middle class. If England has had a backbone, it would surely have been seen in her yeomen. Shakespeare saved the most inspiring lines of Henry V's battle-cry for such men:

> 'And you, good yeomen,
> Whose limbs were made in England, show us here
> The mettle of your pasture – let us swear
> That you are worth your breeding.'

James Nayler was to become the leading Quaker writer of the Friends' formative years, his publications even outnumbering those of George Fox. His skill in argument and address had been widely noticed long before he made the Quaker connection. He had obviously received a fair grounding in the use of English. The Reverend

John Deacon, who was to become one of Nayler's bitterest and most persistent critics, is our surprisingly helpful source of details, getting his information from 'a gentleman, now of that honourable society of Gray's Inn', who claimed to have been Nayler's school-fellow and 'knew his friends'. Notwithstanding prejudice, Deacon allowed Nayler to have been 'a man of exceeding quick wit and sharp apprehension, enriched with that commendable gift of good oratory with a very delightable melody in his utterance'. He can never have been robust, and later developed tubercular symptoms. As it is noticeable that his parents are never mentioned in his writings, it is possible that the chest weakness ran in the family and that they both, or one of them, died young. Neither were any of the family mentioned, except one brother, William. Given the death toll of the day, probably several infants were lost.

A few straight drawings of the mature Nayler survive, besides caricatures and foreign suppositions. Of the two that aspire to char-acter, they are so unlike each other as to defeat credibility. One thing seems certain: he did not look like a typical Yorkshireman – that is, as imagined, a squarely-built figure with an open face, shrewd eyes and capable hands. One that appeared in an engrav-ing from Holland in 1657 has been dubiously ascribed to the school of Rembrandt, and its look of endurance and humanity gives point to that suggestion. 'He had been seeking the way of salvation from a child' we are told. The streak of asceticism must have made him lonely in a farming family, and although James pulled his weight when he was at home, he looked for no other employment when he left, and seems to have cut the old ties of land work willingly enough when a stronger challenge arose.

The decision to send him to school must have been hard for a father whose need for a pair of hands could easily have outweighed his perception of a good brain in this sensitive boy. Whatever the school at Wakefield achieved for James, the seeds of his future eloquence would have been sown by his attendance at church and contact with the minister. Country livings, when not snapped up by the younger sons of the gentry, were already providing a response to the Puritanism that had steadily grown in England since the emotional clean sweep of the Reformation.

In partnership with his spiritual side James had developed a lively interest in politics. He was seven when James I, 'the wisest fool', had been succeeded by the hopeful Prince Charles, who inherited the effects of a continuing Thirty Years War in Europe and had to cope with the resentment of other countries towards a neutral England. 'In another age', a modern historian has remarked, 'Charles I would have been a great reforming monarch.' The 1630's when Nayler was a schoolboy brought treaties that made some parties speak of a golden age, but the royal finances were in desperate straits. The King was levying taxes on all levels of the population that threatened future storms. Inland areas especially resented Ship Money, introduced for the restoration of the fleet, a cause that made little sense to farmers when it no longer carried the appeal of a nation rallying its forces against the Spanish Armada. The royal prerogative was challenged by figures as disparate as the high-minded Hampden and the wily John Pym. Parliament was flexing its muscles and the King, outmanoeuvred, had to sacrifice his unpopular advisers, Archbishop Laud and Strafford.

All these peaks of history on the move would have reached young James through a matching assault on his inward search for reality. The pressures of politics at that time were counter-balanced not only by conflict between forms of religion, between Catholic and Protestant, between Calvinist and Arminian, but by the unseen yet strongly felt spiritual needs that were drawing groups of people together outside the formal church services. James was attracted to a vein of independence in the congregation at Woodchurch, outside his own parish. At the same time he was responding to the equally unsettling attraction of the daughter of one of his near-Wakefield neighbours.

Difficult as it is to be certain of James' looks, there is no evidence whatever to help us identify Anne, who became his wife. If character is any indication she was a Yorkshirewoman through and through, straightforward, realistic, no humbug, and for all her practical nature, compassionate. Their courtship probably took no account of the salient fact that she was exactly the right sort of wife for him. She was to need all her independence and the reserves of loyalty and understanding that lay beneath it. It is noticeable that in the various close researches into James' character and motives his sexual drive has never been considered. It must have been an important force to be reckoned with, feared and resisted in turn by

4

him, but never far from the surface. That he fell deeply in love with Anne is shown clearly enough by the prompt arrival of three daughters in succession immediately following their marriage. James was twenty-one, which was exceptionally young in 1639 for a man to take a wife. The couple acquired a farm of their own, presumably being in a position to pay for it. Their future looked bright, but for the increasing unrest that was threatening to reach its climax in open war. The birth of the third child in 1643 coincided with increased military manoeuvres in Yorkshire.

The parliamentary army was commanded by an outstanding new General, Sir Thomas Fairfax, who launched an attack on Royalist Leeds followed by a bitter confrontation at Wakefield when the castle changed hands twice before yielding to the General, who had to cope with over a thousand Royalist prisoners. The whirl of activity so near to their own land could not fail to engage the Naylers' deep concern. While Anne's chief anxiety was for her young children, James had studied the tensions of Parliament's opposition to the King. The eruption of battle hardly came as a surprise; he was clear where his sympathies lay, and like many of his neighbours he was quickly drawn into the conflict. Fairfax was a Yorkshire campaigner, well known and trusted by Northerners. He had the authority of an old local family behind him: his father, the second Baron Fairfax of Cameron, had also commanded parliamentary forces, chiefly in Yorkshire. The son had an engaging manner with his troops, asking no more of them than he was willing to suffer himself in the way of danger and discomfort. James, who was to serve with this company for seven years, found every opportunity to learn hardship on the road, courage under attack, and understanding of his fellow-troopers.

Though he had had as yet no challenge to his orthodox religious upbringing, there was everywhere in the army of that day, together with belief in their cause, a dedicatory spirit invoking the guidance of God. The driving force of Oliver Cromwell was a new element rapidly coming to the front. Like others in the English Revolution he was a man born into the one hour, or decade, that would use his genius to the full. There would be no one to replace him. His 'inch of taper' would be quickly burnt out. The inspiration that he gave his army of Ironsides owed much of its brightness to the readiness with which they received it. His battle-cry of 'God is our strength' aroused all the latent fervour of the men's resentment against injustice and suspicion that their freedom was being whittled away. As with the leaders, so with the men; the hour created the spirit. In the camps of Cromwell and Fairfax there was a revivalist fervour concentrated into prayer and evangelistic power. It was no wonder that James Nayler in his mid-twenties found himself responding to that atmosphere. He had been awakened to the use of that 'commendable gift of good oratory' that was later to impress his critics.

The spirit of the ranks was to have no time for frivolities and the arts of peace. Poetry was an illegitimate grace, unacknowledged though showing parental features in language plundered from the century's gift of the Bible. James was an unconscious stylist. He was to work hard at his speech and writing, but for now he sprang into a reputation for his extempore sermons that kept his company's devotion to the cause at boiling point. He was something of a treasure to those in command. The men learned to recognize this comrade, 'a man of good complexion, brown hair which he wears of an indifferent length', mainly by his voice, which could use a remarkable range to cast a spell over his audience. He may have looked like a simple countryman, but he was a born communicator, given scope to polish his gifts. It was evidently the voice that brought him to the notice of General John Lambert, who had been a protegé of Fairfax and had distinguished himself in campaigns in Scotland. Lambert was also a Yorkshireman, born at Calton near Skipton, rapidly rising in the New Model Army and in 1647 promoted to command of the Northern Forces. Two years later James found himself transferred to Lambert's Regiment of Horse, being given officer status in the responsible post of Quartermaster.

Life in the army for both sides was a less stirring affair than it has often been depicted. Battles tended to bespatter the maps in spring and summer, after which the reconstituted forces settled themselves into winter quarters for a long wait. Entertainment being out of fashion, religion found a new form for its medieval rôle of magnetising a crowd. As the touring players had done, and parsons had tried to do according to their gifts, certain soldiers' personalities came to the fore and their talents were promoted. Instead of stage visions of heaven and hell, they saw a way of salvation within their grasp, an ideal world that might await them when

the current ordeal was over. They must strive, said these oppor-
tunist preachers, to perfect themselves and be ready to show an
example of a better life. In this forcing-house of eloquence James
Nayler was a natural. His line was never to attack the men for sins
that army life made inevitable, but to show them the transience of
all sin compared with a strong instinct for honesty and truth to
which Christ called them. His words in themselves probably had
less effect than the power of their delivery: he was a star. His
reputation was spreading, and assured him an audience.

In 1650 Lambert's forces joined with Cromwell to oppose
Charles II's landing in Scotland, and in September of that year
came the decisive victory of Parliament at Dunbar. It is to this
period that we owe the only personal report of Nayler's impact on
the troops, a report handed down by chance, charged with such
conviction that it loads his General's reference to his 'exceeding
usefulness' with double meaning. It has to be quoted in full. The
passage appears in the Memoirs of Thomas Gough, published in
1781. It describes how his subject, a worthy Friend named James
Wilson, had in early life 'conceived a very contemptible opinion of
the people called Quakers'. This was obviously shared by a bar
parlour full of voluble drinkers, who were interrupted by the arrival
of a former officer in Cromwell's army, who defended the Quakers
so eloquently that Wilson found the whole of his speech worth pre-
serving. His record went into Gough's memoirs as follows:

> After the Battle of Dunbar, as I was riding in Scotland at the
> head of my troop, I observed at some distance from the road a
> crowd of people, and one higher than the rest. Upon which I
> sent one of my men to see and bring me word what was the
> meaning of this gathering. Seeing him ride up and stay there
> without returning according to my order, I sent a second who
> stayed in like manner, and I then determined to go myself.
> When I came thither, I found it was James Nayler preaching to
> the people, but with such power and reaching energy as I had
> not till then been witness of. I could not help staying a little,
> for I was made a Quaker, being forced to tremble at the sight
> of myself. I was struck with more terror before the preaching
> of James Nayler than I was before the Battle of Dunbar, when
> we had nothing else to expect but to fall a prey to the swords
> of our enemies.

In time the combined effect of cold, damp, frequent marches and exposure to all weathers began to take its toll from a frame predisposed to infection. A cough familiar from childhood became more pronounced. The work of a quartermaster rose and fell with the seasons. On literally active service, such as the crucial Battle of Marston Moor which left four thousand Royalists dead, the corresponding number of prisoners had to be accommodated and fed, horses catered for and visiting divisions sheltered. General Lambert may have found Nayler 'exceedingly useful', but after two years of this effort he had to recognize that his quartermaster's health was failing. 'We parted from him with great regret', said Lambert. Whether James felt equal regret is not known, but in the spring of 1651 he rode back to his farm near Wakefield, an exhausted man.

'James Nayler preaching .... with such power and reaching energy'
(see page 7).

CHAPTER II

Confronting the Light

ANNE NAYLER HAD parted from her husband in full support of his enthusiasm for the cause that seemed to offer the people's ultimate security. She remembered him as a slightly-built but active young man, his half-curling brown hair and shining out-door face turned towards her as he waved farewell. She now saw slower movement from a man in his middle thirties, the slight build turned to spareness, the face tired, perhaps drawn with emotion at the thought of the strangers his family might have become. It is unlikely that the nine years had passed without occasional visits, letters and messages, condensed by the pressure of an army on the move, at odd times finding itself near home. This was different: a man facing re-direction, to be confronted by a self-reliant woman and a brood of growing girls.

She had sensed from his letters that his early optimism had faded. The triumphs of Parliament seemed less and less likely to lead to a land of equal opportunity for all, as the taste of power began to be felt by leaders, especially in Cromwell's case. There were even rumours, following the King's execution, that Oliver could be tempted to accept the crown. James would write to him himself two years later:

> Thus in faithfulness to God and in love to you, with whom I have served for the good of these nations betwixt eight and nine years, counting nothing too dear to bring the government into your hands in whom it is many can witness with me herein, and now my prayer to God for you is that you may lay down all your crowns at his feet who hath crowned you with victory, that so the Lord being set up asking in every conscience, all may be subject to your government for conscience sake.

9

The views of John Lilburne and the Levellers, and those of Gerrard Winstanley, who had led famished country workers to take over the waste land that might nourish their children, had been much discussed in the army. Their hopes and sufferings had a permanent effect on James, though the stand he was to take was on different ground from theirs. Undoubtedly Cromwell's crushing attack on the Levellers at Burford Bridge had helped to build up his questioning of authority. He now returned to the seasonal routines of farm life almost with a sense of relief, but unable to relax the bonds of an inward struggle that was the permanent legacy of the religious experience fostered in the army. He was aware that his own very active part in those spiritual challenges had made radical changes in his character.

For his wife there was from that time onward an element of mystery present in him that would test her loyalty almost to its limit. For the present all she could do was to make him feel needed once again by his family, to care for him unobtrusively without urging too much work on his overstrained body, and to look to the future in a country that had gone through unimaginable changes since their marriage. She found that although he tried to work as though nothing had happened, he was often abstracted in thoughts that tore him away from the old routines. As peak periods approached workers needed engaging at the local market. This had fallen on Anne for years past. She tried to trust him to take charge, but felt deeply anxious. Her hope at that stage was in the influence of the church which had attracted him before he went away, and James was soon welcomed there.

Woodchurch had a new minister, Christopher Marshall, a man of notable experience for a country pastor. A Cambridge-educated scholar from Lincolnshire, he had faced the certain dangers and discomforts of a voyage to America to study under a renowned Puritan preacher, John Cotton. On his safe return to England, thus qualified, it is surprising to find him consigned to the then remote West Riding with a salary of £30 a year from the patron, the Earl of Sussex. An accomplished speaker, he found his rural congregation often augmented by returned soldiers such as James Nayler.

Later in the year topics of conversation throughout the northern counties had begun to concentrate on the highly expressive, irrepressible, provocative company of proselytes known as Quakers, recruited from individual groups of seekers by the youthful whirl-wind George Fox. Visiting some of these in the Doncaster area Fox was advised that there would be a fruitful ground for his message around Wakefield, and that he would be likely, as once before, to get a foothold in the house of one Lieutenant Roper, lately of the parliamentary army. James Nayler was a familiar figure in that home, near to his own farm. He and Roper had known each other in the ranks and had no doubt had many debates on the probable direction of the churches, then in a dangerous state of confusion. On Fox's arrival the Ropers hosted a meeting to give local church supporters an opportunity to meet the now noted free-thinker.

This scrambled event that brought Fox and Nayler face to face could scarcely have looked like a moment of destiny to either of them, but it was clear to Fox that here was a convert worth win-ning, while to Nayler the very gaze of the young iconoclast demanded an instant response. Fox's hypnotic power and the shin-ing persuasion of his eyes had at that time reached their first and perhaps fullest self-confidence. James had already met men from his own region who had been drawn into the Quaker advancement, including William Dewsbury from the West Riding who had brought his wife Ann to this meeting. Dewsbury had won Nayler's affection from the first with his open nature and the fervour of his search for truth. He too was fresh from the army and now shared with James the experience that was to transform life for them both.

Fox held the floor in Roper's parlour and proceeded to under-mine every tenet, custom and support of the organized churches they had formerly believed in but had begun to question. He flashed out his scorn on ministers who could accept stipends for practis-ing their religion, and urged his hearers to refuse what he called the extortionate habit of paying tithes to those who should have offered their faith freely. He had left his Leicestershire home and devout parents, had wandered through towns and villages drawing their pastors into exhaustive debate and finding no answers that would satisfy his devouring need for a genuine approach to God. He told them of his final despair, and how he had said 'When all my hopes were gone, then, Oh then, I heard a voice which said, "There is one, even Jesus Christ, that can speak to thy condition", and when I heard it, my heart did leap for joy'. He had discovered, as he said, the direct way to grace, faith and power. There was no need for a secondary agent, paid or unpaid. No need for a human interpreter.

His approach to the 'hireling priests', sometimes in their own 'steeple-houses', ('Come down, thou deceiver!' was a fairly typical attack), and his interruptions of their services, had not surprisingly brought rough treatment upon himself and reaction from the law. Several times in that early stage of his ministry he had learned for himself the conditions of seventeenth century prisons. The courts took small account of the degrees of crime; murderers, petty thieves and blasphemers, in which class Fox was often accused, were all thrust into the fumes of airless holes and left to the variable mercies of jailers who might or might not allow food to be brought in for them, according to their whims or the prisoner's means. He had spent the greater part of 1651, before his first meeting with Nayler, in Derby Jail, which had become a focal point for the mounting devotion of those already reached by him. It was in Derby that the name of Quaker, used in mocking reference to Fox's advice that his opponents should learn to quake before God's judgment, had begun to attach itself to his infant community of Friends. On his release several personalities soon to be well known as his followers were drawn into the cause – the fiery Richard Farnsworth, Thomas Aldam who had already felt the fresh breeze of Quakerism, and the Killam brothers who brought their enthusiastic wives into the movement.

It was becoming natural for couples to work together, wives testifying at meetings, or even travelling alone. Because of this, it was noticeable that Anne Nayler stayed at home while this seminal meeting took place. The answer seems to have been that she had decided on her rôle as the fixed anchorage in James' unpredictable life. She had sensed that the farm was a stopgap for him but would never satisfy the urge of mind and heart that willed him to join George Fox. His first departure, dictated by events, had shaped her character over the years into a healthy independence as the mainstay of the family. She would never relax her readiness to go to his help in extremity, but it remained a hidden tension while she moved to the rhythms of work and home.

As George talked, James compared his past life under military control with the freedom exercised by this young man at his own choice. Fox's needs were obviously few, but served with good sense:

leather suiting for hard wear, a broad-brimmed hat against sun and rain, a workaday horse accustomed to all weathers, a trained ability to snatch sleep as easily under a haystack or in the stocks as in the luxury of an occasional bed. On his own admission George had money in his pocket, probably supplied from home, and good clean linen to wear which was sometimes pulled out to demonstrate to the law that he could not be sentenced as a vagrant. With rare intermissions George had good health and extraordinary physical endurance. James on the other hand would not have been invalided home after his good record in the army without serious concern, and the sound of his tubercular cough was eloquent proof. He remembered his regular pay increasing to four shillings a day as quartermaster, and realized that he could not be subsidised by Anne as an out-of-work evangelist; she had enough responsibilities already. George was a younger man by six years, fresh from his first experience of an overriding inspiration to service; James had responded nine years earlier to the call for what had promised to be a better world, and by way of disillusionment had reached the point of exhaustion.

These were legitimate doubts – and yet – as George reached the heart of his message, something miraculously young and untried went directly to an answering spirit in his listeners, and above all to a still unrecognized vein of power in James Nayler. He was hearing for the first time, regardless of the countless sermons he had performed so effectively himself, that there was in his own being an inward light, unquenchable, fed by genesis itself before hand was conceived or voice heard, a clear guidance with no material source, strengthened by the example of the life of Jesus and available to every man or woman who took its counsel against the world's argument. Given the difference in their characters it was possible that this revelation struck James with more mixed feelings than it had embodied for Fox, its contemporary re-discoverer, because for George, the tougher fighter, its clarity could never be obscured by others' reasoning. The heightened sensibility of James carried the incipient danger that he could allow for an apparent similarity in the testimony around him, to his own cost.

George had come on a few miles detour to the Ropers from the firming Quaker centre at Balby where he could be sure of a welcome from stalwarts such as Farnsworth. When these had directed him to Roper's house it was likely that he had been told of the spell-binding preacher lately retired from the army who was living near by. This would explain the brevity of the note in his *Journal* that he 'went into the country about Wakefield where James Nayler lived, where he was convinced'. The latter word was Fox's shorthand for a man's soul bowled over by his eloquence. The phrase 'where James Nayler lived' suggests a lingering breath of fame attached to the former soldier.

George had met Roper and his wife before. The man was 'almost a Friend', but remained in that category, and Mistress Roper was a lively effusive character given to throwing her arms round a visitor with a resounding kiss. George, as her temporary house guest, could watch with a wry smile as she bestowed this greeting on her interesting neighbour James Nayler, with particular relish in the absence of his wife. It is possible that Anne, a woman of a different mould, had little taste or time for visiting at the Ropers. At all events the kiss from his hostess was destined to take a sinister part in future charges against James.

That particular kiss, however interpreted, meant little to James at the time in comparison with his surrender to Fox's message. All the causes of the deep depression that had haunted him since his loss of faith in human government had been swept away by a conviction that would soon cause him to write:

> That faith which we own and witness is that which stands in Jesus Christ the everlasting covenant of light who is the light of the world and hath enlightened everyone that cometh into the world, and this light we believe and follow, and by this we are led out of all the ways, works and worships of this dark world.

He carried a new hope in his heart as he went home that night, and at the same time a tumult of overturned habits of mind. Where would this discovery lead? Must he go out into the world like Fox to promote the inward light for those who owned it without being aware? As he looked at his sleeping children there was bitterness in his thoughts for all the years when he had hardly known them. The eldest girl seemed almost a woman already. Anne was busy with the next morning's dues. In the style of their day she was approaching middle age. Could he look her in the face and break such news?

For the time being there was a refuge in his solitary work out in the fields, where he could find quietness to still the conflict in his mind. If he imagined that an interval had been granted for his temporary withdrawal from the challenging spirit, he was soon to be reawakened. The moment from which there could be no retreat is best described in his own words in an answer he gave in the following year to his judges in a court of law:

> I was at the plough, meditating on the things of God, and suddenly I heard a voice saying unto me, Get thee out from thy kindred, and from thy father's house. And I had a promise given in with it. Whereupon I did exceedingly rejoice, that I had heard the voice of that God which I had possessed from a child, but had never known him.

He would go on to explain that while under the immediate impact of that voice he had gone home, made over all his possessions to his family and arranged for any money owed by or accruing to him to be transferred to them. (It is believed that a son had been born at an unknown date.) This prompt action was followed, as he tried to bring himself to the actual point of farewells and final departure, by a revulsion so violent that he was reduced to a trance of indecision. The body, already weakened by the sickness that had brought him home, could not support the demand of the will. 'The wrath of God was upon me', as he expressed it, 'I was made a wonder to all, and none thought I would have lived.'

No speculation has survived as to Anne Nayler's feelings on the prospect in front of her. She seemed to have won him back from one imminent death to be faced with the likelihood of another; for that is what her practical nature foresaw of his chances if he went off, without money or goods, to the sort of life reputed to be lived by the Quakers. We can believe, even with the spontaneity demanded by the Almighty, that James on his return from his visionary call had discussed it with his wife. The arrangement about the money would have implied as much. She was certain of one thing: if God said he must go, he would go. She knew James. This seemed to be an even more undeniable urge than the one that sent him, in the prime of youth and health, into the Great Rebellion. With a heavy heart she saw the little girls off to the village dame-school, the eldest having got up early to do the chores that a farm economy needed. She wondered if it would be wise, even if feasible, to

15

give the boy the sort of education James had had. It might lead....
But Anne turned her thoughts to the matter in hand. He was reviving, and trying to tell her something about another gathering at the
Ropers. Dewsbury and other Friends would be there. George Fox
was coming again. He, James, must be there too. She protested: in
his condition she thought one meeting with Fox was quite enough.
The volatile Mistress Roper was not mentioned, but Anne knew
very well that the pale brooding hero was attractive to many of her
neighbours.

He went, of course. The quietest of their horses took him, and
jibbed a little at the sight of other horses tethered by the Ropers'
gate. It was early summer, and the door to the parlour stood open.
Fox's resounding voice, addressing an audience, came to him as he
walked up the path. An echo, almost a groaning, pressed the words
down into the speaker's throat and soared upwards again so
that James could picture his powerful glance beyond the crowd to
the guiding strength that he believed made short work of any contradiction. James knew that effect on an audience. He had worked
on it himself often enough to recognize, with a tingle of envy, a
master-speaker in full spate. He went inside and found larger numbers than had been there before. From the nods that passed between
them some were familiar with points the speaker was making. But
now George was talking to the strangers. There was one who
insisted on an explanation of some habits by which a man could
be identified as a Quaker.

'Why do you talk of hat-honour? What is it?'

It was held by priests and officers, George told him, that men
removed their hats as a token of respect to mortal authority. Friends
claimed that that honour was due only to God.

'And why do you deny oaths, and refuse to swear?'

The Bible was called in as witness. 'Swear not at all, but let
your yea be yea, and your nay nay.'

It was then alleged that Friends worshipped without the authority of creed, church or sacrament. How could that be called
religion? There was impatience, almost contempt, in Fox's reply.
When Quakers said they believed in that of God in man, this was
essentially religious. It required no intermediary, or sacred building, or hireling priest, to make human echoes of the voice of God.

16

James heard no more that day. He went home with a strengthening of the summons that had come to him in the fields, but with an obstinate pull of longing for the well-earned retreat with his wife and family. It was no easy conflict to decide; it still threatened his life and sanity. Again he recorded the uncertainty of the passing weeks as his strength returned. 'After I was made willing' – the phrase covers the final struggle – 'I began to make some preparation, as Apparel and other Necessaries, not knowing whither I should go.' So far, so sensible. 'But shortly afterward' – and the narrative is taken over by amazement as though another hand had seized the pen:

....going agateward with a Friend from my own house, having on an old suit, without any money, having neither taken leave of Wife or Children, I was commanded to go into the West, not knowing whither I should go nor what I was to do there; but when I had been there a little while, I had given me what I was to declare, and ever since I have remained not knowing, what I was to do to-morrow.

In the end it was total surrender. The 'necessaries' were left where Anne had supplied them. The home, the respect of a community, the Sunday suit, the loves and frustrations of family life, all fell away. Except in the rôle of a visitor, he would never see them again.

James looking at his sleeping children (see page 14).

CHAPTER III

Swarthmoor

HE WOULD NOT HAVE been human if he had ridden away in a state of euphoria from having so literally obeyed God's command. It is likely that his hard-won willingness was still competing with a sense of sorrow and loss, and concern for those left behind. There can be a crisis in one's life when ruthlessness is the only solution. A quick cut can be made, and the cost counted afterwards. The expression used most often to describe Nayler's face is 'a deep melancholy'. It was imprinted on him now, perhaps with a haunting sense of guilt at having abandoned a partner to whom he already owed so much.

It was a mercy that his illness and his sudden departure had kept from him the news that had spread round the neighbourhood of Christopher Marshall's parish. While still in the area, Fox had gone into the church and listened to Marshall's sermon, at the end of which he stood up and proclaimed 'the word of life' which he claimed had been stifled by the preacher's eloquence. Something of a riot followed, for Marshall was popular. The congregation, outraged, threw the intruder out into the churchyard, threatening to put him in the stocks. It may have been Marshall himself who restrained them. Fox got away unscathed, recalling with some pride 'This was the greatest professor in Yorkshire, but the truth came over all'.

The incident had a bitter consequence for Anne Nayler and her family. Their pastor, already solving the problem of Nayler's absence by connecting it with stories that he had joined the despised Quakers, now officially excommunicated James from what was called 'a very sweet society of an Independent Church'. As he had virtually removed himself, and his address was unknown, the veto meant nothing to its subject who was to hear of it much later, but his family found that they were forbidden to do business with members of the church, or even to eat or drink with them. A suspicion had been aroused that Fox's influence over Nayler had been tainted with witchcraft, a very real menace at that period. Marshall himself gave credence to the stories, as Fox related with relish,

> that I carried bottles and made people drink of them, which made them follow me; and that I rid of a great black horse, and was seen in one country upon it in one hour, and at the same hour in another country threescore miles; and that I would give a fellow money to follow me, when I was on my black horse. With these hellish lies he fed his people, to make them think evil of the truth which I had declared amongst them.

He added in triumph 'I was then travelling on foot, and had no horse at that time', and finally disposed of his adversary as he so often did, but in this case being somewhat misled: 'The Lord not long after cut off this envious priest in his wickedness.'

James would have dealt with the whole matter somewhat differently. It is sad to know that, unlike George, he left no journal of his life, though from that time onward he never lacked friends whose surviving letters have given vivid touches about his work and the affection he obviously inspired. From Richard Farnsworth comes proof that James was visiting his home during July; he wrote to 'My dear Friend James Nayler at his house at Wakefield Woodside'. It was in Farnsworth's company that James paid many of the challenging visits to places in Yorkshire that kept him busy during that summer. The two may have given the impression of fire and calming water, for while Farnsworth wrote 'I have had two set meetings with the priests and they are even teared to pieces: the sword is sharp, the rider active, the armour proved... Down, down they fall' – a fair image of his technique – Nayler, equally certain of his aim, used a natural courtesy in verbal sparring. A significant point from Farnsworth's record in view of Nayler's later experience, is that some of his hearers had issued warrants against him for blasphemy after he had alleged that he, Farnsworth, was the light of the world. This was a charge that was made fairly regularly against Friends at that time without spectacular consequences.

This early friendship was a lasting one, but in the meantime James was eager for more contact with Fox, who was travelling further north. Hearing that he was speaking in the Furness area they turned westward and finally caught up with him at Swarthmoor Hall, where the household of Judge Fell, magistrate and prominent local dignitary, had been dramatically wrought upon in the Judge's absence by George's visit.

Furness, like a turned-down thumb from the extended palm of Lakeland, seems to have been a forgotten country in comparison with the exalted traditions of its neighbour. Travellers in the seventeenth century usually had to cross the dangerous sands of Morecambe Bay before they came to the grey stone manor house of Swarthmoor, a little to the south of Ulverston. Quakers seem to have found a natural home in the area, which is littered with surviving or former Meeting Houses. At the time of the earliest Friends' assault its remoteness was emphasised by the fact that like the rest of rural England it was mostly self-governing, the judges, sheriffs and constables being locally appointed and unpaid. Roads were little more than stone or mud-tracks, and the rare coaches could scarcely depend on covering 80 miles in three days. Ministers of the church had their stipends and tithes, and perhaps more power than at any other time in history, despite the vast number of sects that gnawed at their authority.

The Fell family had an easy relationship with its vicar, William Lampitt, who came and went freely at the Hall whether the owners were at home or not, knowing that travellers from any branches of the Christian church were equally warmly received. He little knew, when George Fox arrived in the Fells' absence, that his friendly hand would be held out to one who was an implacable and avowed critic of all organized religion. George quickly made that plain, and wrote in his *Journal* 'He would have owned me, but I could not own him nor join with him, he was so full of filth'. Six young daughters of the Fells, and one son, crowded in to listen to this full-blooded exchange of views, and from an epistle to Mr Lampitt written by one of them aged eight, it appears that George's style was catching:

Lampitt the plaiges of god shall fall upon thee, and the seven viols (sic) shall bee powerd upon thee, and the milstone shall fall upon thee, and crush thee as dost under the lords feete how

Can thou escape the damnation of hell. This did the lord give mee as I lay in bed: Mary ffell.

The vicar's discomfited exit was followed by the return of Mistress Fell herself, who realized, as Fox confronted her, that this was no wandering preacher of the sort who had so often sought shelter at Swarthmoor. In the whole history of his ministry Fox was to have no more ardent disciple than Margaret Fell. This commanding woman, already distinguished in manner and outlook, saw the former shepherd-boy and shoemaker from the East Midlands, described much later by the ex-courtier William Penn as sounding 'uncouth and unfashionable to nice ears', as in truth he was to appear to Penn 'an original, being no man's copy'. Their relationship, in Margaret Fell's case as in Penn's, had an element of the attraction of opposites. She never ceased to be magnetised by the directness of Fox, his certainty, after initial confusion, that the only true guidance was given by God to each individual, and his often ruthless way of dealing with opposition. There was, from the days of his earliest strivings within himself, a dash of vanity in Fox which perhaps he had failed to count among the devils that beset him. The priest of his home town had praised him, but George noted 'What I said in discourse to him in the week-days he would preach of in the first-days; for which I did not like him'. This touchiness could be lost on Margaret Fell in the abundance of his confidence. She not only spread her belief in him over her entire family (only resisted by the son as he grew up) but devoted her home to the comfort of his often bruised and bleeding supporters, and made herself the focal point of a correspondence with them all that would be a mine of information to posterity, not always quite without prejudice.

Some days went by during which Fox made a base at Swarthmoor for his various visits in the district. He was away at the time of Nayler's and Farnsworth's arrival, and it was they who first confronted a fairly irate Judge Fell, newly returned from weeks of duty on the Welsh circuit, and from listening to the ready tongues from far and near who assailed him with their versions of scandalous goings-on at the Hall. Thomas Fell, upon whose attitude the freedom and encouragement of the whole household depended, was neither a tyrant nor an indifferent or dominated husband. He wanted a reasonable explanation of the worrying rumours. His wife had been bewitched by an intruder with devilish arts, his children forced out of their usual games and lessons, including their music, and his well-known and respected minister confounded in argument and driven into retreat. It was a considerable account to be settled, and Margaret may have found that she was lucky to have a newcomer like James Nayler, experienced in moments of crisis, to step in as a catalyst more effectively than George Fox might have done. On this occasion Farnsworth, who had learned to know Nayler well, would have kept his usually combative spirit under control to allow the new man to handle the situation.

There is no record of that conversation, but Judge Fell developed a warm regard for the former quartermaster and often enquired about him in his letters home. By the time Fox joined them later that evening the foundations had been laid for that special relationship between the Judge and the Quakers that was no less important than his wife's active concern. He remained his own man, never a declared Friend, but playing a vital part in their defence. There was a certain parallel to be drawn between his position and Anne Nayler's.

Fox came in to find that instead of pacifying another opponent he had only to supply what he called 'a great opening', with an exercise of his most dazzling eloquence, to convince the Judge that his way of revelation was well founded. George was in remarkable form that evening. He had more than one appreciative listener: James was discovering the full extent of the love and admiration that Fox could inspire.

On leaving Swarthmoor George and James had their first opportunity of working together. Fox had a leading towards Walney Island, having recently had some success in that long bracket of land enclosing Lower Furness. He took Nayler with him. It was a chance for each of them of some degree of intimacy. As they rode, and as they spent a night at an inn before making the crossing, they exchanged views and made estimates of each other: two exceptional men who would soon find themselves with a problem – who was the real leader? This was the period in which the definite principles associated with Friends were still in the process of development. Young George had framed his own witness against war and all 'outward weapons' (in which he presumably did not include belligerent views on paper). They were fairly well formed and would allow his sturdy physique to take savage beatings without response. He explained to Nayler the underlying conviction, amounting to an animating dream, that would bring about the world of communicated love that God had hopefully implanted within the power of every human being. As so many of his newly-won followers had come from a divinely-inspired army, his common sense – with which George's visions were always seasoned – told him that it would be useless to rush them into a resolution that would be like and yet unlike their former ideals. He knew his path. They must find theirs. Most of them did. To Nayler it was a path aflame with his new friend's inspiration, though he scarcely realized how soon the principle was to be tested.

Fox had been glad to count another ex-soldier, an educated man and a ready writer, among his 'convincements' in Yorkshire. He welcomed the new Friend's spirituality, and felt he could rely on gifts honed and liberally applied in the New Model Army. He could not avoid noticing the speed with which his followers, wherever groups of them were found, were taking Nayler to their hearts and gladly offering help to him; he was rapidly becoming 'the dear James Nayler', a style of reference already attached to him. Whether George ever felt the same love for James as other Friends did is less clear than James' whole-hearted response to his companion's magnetism. Not long after the Walney Island journey he was writing to George with almost breathless devotion: 'My father, my father, the glory of Israel, my heart is ravished with thy love above what can be declared. Let me live in thy bosom as a seal set upon thy heart for ever.' James had, as would be evidenced much later, the makings of a poet, which now overflowed under the influence of the Psalms. For the present, what his rapturous declaration proved was that the strange adventure into which he had been so abruptly launched was producing an almost light-headed happiness in him. Fox was the main source and promoter of this, he felt. Fox on the other hand unhesitatingly ascribed every advantage that came his way to the favour ordained for him by God. A jealous God, too, who obviously only saw one side of a question and had no time for 'jangling Baptists' and other fools who got in George's way.

When writing his *Journal* in years to come he tended to magnify the Lord's triumphs and belittle the opposition, but the population of Furness and Walney Island gave the two reforming preachers a rough ride. Before they had even embarked on the crossing to Walney a man at one of their meetings attempted to fire a pistol at Fox, and on landing on the island they were violently attacked with every weapon that came to hand. Fox was left senseless and came round to find his latest convert, James Lancaster, attempting to shield him from the blows of an irate wife. Nayler, so long trained to fight back, found the ardent welcome he had given to George's pacifist views abruptly shaken by this attack on his companion. Knowing that George would firmly reject any physical support, but feeling unable to stand by and watch such a scene, he rushed into a nearby field and was extremely sick. James Lancaster, having taken most of the blows from his wife intended for George, managed to get him into a boat and row him back to the mainland. Nayler had reappeared and the frustrated crowd turned its fury on him. With yells of 'Kill him! Kill him!' they quickly reduced the unprotesting victim to the same bruised and bleeding state as his friend, linking him with Fox as suspected practisers of witchcraft.

Fox, back on the mainland at the house of supporters, sent one of them over to look for Nayler, and the two injured men were given first aid before their return to Swarthmoor the next morning. While they were still recovering Judge Fell came home from another spell of duty to find that a warrant was being prepared to arrest Fox for blasphemy. He took measures to prevent its issue, but George could not be dissuaded from going to Lancaster Sessions to answer the charge, warrant or no warrant.

There followed one of those curious instances of the eccentricity of legal processes at that time. Fox and Nayler could be observed riding to the Sessions in the company of Judge Fell who was about to sit on the bench with their accusers, to be met by an equally sympathetic Colonel West who had heard of Fox's challenge and now smiled upon him with the jovial greeting 'What, are you come into the dragon's mouth?'

An array of no less than forty outraged parish priests confronted them, lined up behind the strongly anti-Quaker Justice Sawyer. They were not slow to unleash their basic anxiety that the Quaker condemnation of tithes and paid ministry, if encouraged, would result in savage cuts in their income: a natural enough concern.

Unfortunately for them it had to be masked by a polemical debate, in which their case was weakened by too many of them being eager to put in an argument.

This was a field in which George Fox was more than a match for them. He quickly produced witnesses who proved that the priests had accused him of statements such as declaring himself to be equal with God, a claim he had never been heard to utter. A vital matter to the Quakers was the reliance of church ministers on 'the Letter' (ie. the sacred words of the Bible) being identified with 'the Spirit' (which in a Quaker's view was the direct guidance of God). The priests protested that spirit and letter were inseparable. If that is the case, George told them, God could be sold in the market as one might buy a copy of the Bible. By this time the Quakers were winning, and Colonel West, who was obviously enjoying himself, stood up and said that if George wished to speak to the public he could declare it 'in the open Sessions'. It was a small triumph for the defendants and their Friends in the court.

The increasingly well-known music of James Nayler's voice had seldom been heard in these proceedings, but he was realizing that he had much to learn from Fox and that his role at present was to be seen as supporter. He was beginning to recognize George's style as he described the collapse of the priests as 'like an old rotten house... and the cry was amongst all people far and near that the Quakers had got the day and that the priests were fallen' – a typically Foxian example of the wish being father to the thought. It was at this time that Nayler was observing how the practice of fasting had been used by George to concentrate his mind on the Truth. George obviously found it beneficial, and it did no harm to his usual robust health, but there were dangers in it for James, who was to resort to fasting at times of pressure and uncertainty. His constitution, undermined by the weakness of his lungs, was in no state to risk starvation.

They had separate commitments after the Lancaster episode. Nayler had been invited to speak to Friends at Kendal, and there he had an encounter that both tested his firmness in the Quaker cause and gave proof of the standing he had already gained. Word of his visit had gone round the town, and after the meeting with Friends he was waylaid by two priests who had enlisted the support of local magistrates. An 'exceeding great multitude' was gathering out of curiosity to hear how the rising celebrity would deal with the situation. A resounding voice accustomed to the echoes of a church hailed him, as from an avenging angel: 'Nayler, I have a message from the Lord Jesus Christ unto thee!' but unwisely added that they were not in a convenient place for it. James seized the opening with an inviting gesture: 'The Lord Jesus Christ is no respecter of places.' So the message was delivered on the main road into the town. They would know 'by what power thou inflictest such punishment upon the bodies of creatures?' James reminded the speaker of Christ's answer to such a demand, and added 'If thou hast the spirit of God, as thou sayest thou hast, then thou canst tell by what power it is done'.

Shifting his ground, the priest rashly challenged the Quakers' belief in an inward light, declaring that not everybody could possess it. James said 'Put out one in all this great multitude that dare say he hath it not'.

'Ah,' said the priest, 'but these are Christians. If a Turk or Indian were here, he would deny it.'

James, feeling that he had the crowd on his side, teased him a little. 'Thou goest far for a proof, but if a Turk were here he would witness against thee.'

The priest's party turned away, sensing trouble, and James called after them 'These are thy Christians, and this is the fruits of thy ministry'.

Stung to fury, they followed him as far as the bridge and threatened to throw him over the parapet. At this stage the Friend who reported the scene saw a surge of confidence in James. 'The word of the Lord came to him.' He spoke to the crowd in such strength that he and his supporters were seen on their way unscathed.

He had reason to feel confident by now, but a further test awaited him. Turning northward to Orton, after much rough handling he was accused in an alehouse, by a Justice and a priest, of the by now familiar Quaker provocations of disrespectful speech to superiors ('thee' and 'thou' being reserved for one's social equals) and of refusing to take off his hat. Adding a charge of vagrancy on the grounds that nobody in the town could vouch for him, this unofficial court summoned a guard and proceeded to commit him for trial at the Sessions in the county town of Appleby.

James had recognized the once-familiar face of Arthur Scaife, an old soldier, in the bar, and called out to him 'Thou knowest me! I was in the army with thee eight or nine years'.

Before the man could answer the Justice dealt with him regardless of logic. 'It is no matter. Thou art no soldier now.'

They then 'carried him to Kirkby Stephen', a dogleg route to take for Appleby, 'and shut him up in a chamber'.

A number of Friends had followed him, and began speaking to the people, which further alarmed the priests. Among these speakers the dominant voice was heard of one who was to be a close associate of Nayler throughout his swinging fortunes. Francis Howgill, born like James in 1618 and convinced by Fox after excoriating ventures into various faiths in his early years, was already a leader among northern Friends. The priests, seeing his effect on the gathering crowd, sent guards out to arrest him. His hat was forcibly removed and hurled into the fire, and the two Quakers, thrown together into a village lock-up under supervision by eight assembled constables – a situation of Gilbertian propensities – passed the night more companionably than either of them had expected, sowing the seeds of their future friendship.

The following morning, still under guard, they were taken the ten remaining miles to Appleby Jail.

James Lancaster's wife stoning George Fox in 1652, despite her husband's protection. James Nayler was accompanying Fox and was attacked on the same day (see top of page 24).

CHAPTER IV

To London

AMONG ENGLISH PRISONS during the Commonwealth, Appleby holds a special place in Quaker history for cruelty and deprivation towards its captives. Nayler and Howgill were to spend five months incarcerated there, for the result of the Kendal trial which should have set them free did not satisfy the priests who were their real accusers. The justices, with one or two exceptions, seem to have adopted a more tolerant attitude, and took steps to improve the prison conditions. Ink and paper were among the concessions enjoyed, and the cell at Appleby became James' workroom. It was here that he went into full production of many principal tracts and defences of the Quaker position, some of them, by correspondence, in partnership with George Fox. Margaret Fell recorded that the prisoners were not allowed a fire, and that James, probably from choice, was living on bread and water. Margaret sent him £2 from the relief fund kept at Swarthmoor: he used only five shillings for his own expenses.

After the Lancaster Sessions the accusing party, incensed by the Quakers' victory, had sent a petition to the Council of State in London repeating the charges. Ironically, through a lapse in payment of expenses, this never reached the Council, which only received the spirited answer sent by Fox and Nayler with the title 'Saul's Errand to Damascus'. James had then got hold of a copy of the priests' petition and worked over their main points with a view to publishing a firm denial.

In the opposite camp they were making great efforts to enlarge on accusations that had already been made against James that his marriage had broken down as a result of a liaison with Mistress

Roper. The warmth of that sociable kiss had lost nothing by repetition of alleged onlookers' reports. Messengers were being sent to Wakefield to interview the neighbours, or those of Priest Marshall's congregation already set into a flutter by Nayler's excommunication. His opponents were, as he realized, uncertain of what line to take, and as he said:

> The offence is yet to create.... They have raised many filthy slanders upon me, but I am at peace with my God which hath much appeared unto me since I came into this place, and hath assured me that he will not leave me, neither shall any prevail against me to do me hurt.

This assurance was greatly strengthened by a happening that must have seemed like a miracle to James. The jailer, who had been harsh to the prisoners, put his head close to the grating to inform them that Mistress Nayler, with her two brothers, was at the gate but would not be allowed to visit her husband. The news swept over James in a torrent of mixed feelings: guilt, incredulity, almost dread at the prospect of their meeting. Had she come with reproaches, with demands for an explanation of the rumours of 'filthy slanders', if such they were, that must have reached her? Then the remembrance of her loyalty, and the long-suppressed need of her presence, overcame the doubts. He had an ally: the jailer's wife had been sympathetic all along to the prisoners. Whether it was Nayler's charm or Howgill's persuasiveness, she could be induced by a special plea to use her influence.

So it came about that the massive key turned and Anne Nayler, fresh air clinging to her short fustian jacket, came to confront her husband. The moment can be brought to life through his own words, in a letter to Fox:

> The coming over of my wife was very serviceable and hath stopped many mouths, and hath convinced them of many lies they had raised.... and I myself had great refreshment of her coming for she came and returned, with much freedom and great joy, beyond what I in reason could expect, but I see she was sent of my father and fitted by him not to be in the least a hinderer but a fartherer of his works.

There is immense relief in these expressions, and perhaps a feeling that if only he had confided in her before he left home, there might not have been that abrupt and painful parting.

Anne's practical spirit was indeed 'serviceable'. She had spoken her mind to everyone concerned in spreading rumours about James, and had impressed the judges with her belief that he was innocent of the charges of immorality. This might have been a conspicuous feature of the forthcoming trial, and in fact it appeared to have been dropped in favour of the now-familiar anti-Quaker indictment of the prisoners for blasphemy, for questioning faith in the Bible as written, and for not removing their hats. The last point was answered by Nayler early in the trial with his customary courtesy:

> I do it not in contempt of authority, for I honour the power as it is of God, without respecting men's persons.... Where God commands one thing and man another, I am to obey God rather than man.

This disarming reply ensured that his hat remained firmly in place to the end of the proceedings.

The most significant outcome of this trial for the Quaker movement was the deep impression made on the judges by James' description of having literally heard the voice of God commanding him to go forth then and there from his home and place himself under divine guidance. He brought the radiance of his experience into touching reality, aided no doubt by the tried and proven effect of his oratory. The magistrates were well used to apocalyptic language, but this had a directness that shook them. One said 'I never heard such a call as this in our time'. Said Nayler: 'I believe thee.'

An example of the strange freaks of authority at that time was the presence on the bench of Gervase Benson, who as a Westmorland Seeker had listened to Fox's inspired address from Firbank Fell. A former Mayor of Kendal and holder of numerous offices, he had rejected titles and had already declared himself to be a plain Friend.

A more startling conversion appeared to be the instant effect of Nayler's testimony on Justice Anthony Pearson whose home at Rampshaw Hall was to become, at a crucial period, a second Swarthmoor to Friends in the north-east. Perhaps the varying sympathies of the judges had less weight than the power of the priests, to whom Nayler and Fox, the Quaker movement's leaders, were instruments of the Devil. To them Nayler's views, now appearing in print, were dangerous. Did he not say 'He is no wise man who will leave the light of Christ that once knows it, to follow another man's opinion; and seeing every man would have this liberty in himself, why should he deny it to his brother?' There was no doubt that this man had been under the influence of the Levellers. Justice Benson had come to the conclusion that the prisoner's words were 'neither within the Act against Blasphemy, nor against any law'. Others, dissenting, concentrated on the points raised in the priests' petition, insisting that these should be answered, and on those grounds Nayler and Howgill were sent back to prison until their replies could be accepted.

James settled himself without delay to the task in hand. It was a way of passing the time that gave him useful practice in the Quaker style of defying the established church on paper, and would not only – for once – do what the law required of him but could give the Friends outside welcome copy for their pamphlet crusade. The jailer's well-disposed wife was not only getting the prison conditions eased but obviously obliging with writing materials. While James had been at Swarthmoor his pen had seen good service, and one of his early Quaker contacts in Yorkshire had sent him a gift of an inkhorn 'for my dear brother James Nayler'. These copious writings were the first evidence of the wider fame that was coming to the new leader. During his five years as an active Friend he was to produce thirty-six published works, not including those in collaboration with others, an output well in advance of the general, even those by Fox.

Meanwhile the jailer had begun to reassert himself – one hopes his wife did not have to pay too dearly for her kindness – and the captives were told they would be put in irons and thrust into the underground dungeons. This threat came to nothing as the judges had read a final summing-up by Fox and Nayler under the title 'Several Petitions Answered, that were put up by the Priests of Westmorland'. It appeared to have swept the board clear of the clerical objections. James and Francis were free to fight 'the Lamb's War' over again, out in the open.

Much of the attention of these early Friends was directed to a belief that by living in faithful subjection to the guidance of the Inward Light human beings could testify to that perfection in themselves planted by God at birth but not fully realized. 'Their gospel is Jesus Christ the Lamb of God' wrote James. 'None can witness redemption further than Christ is revealed in them, to set them free from sin, which Christ I witness to be revealed in me in measure.' That proviso of 'measure' was a divining spirit to James throughout his ministry, the key to the essential humility of the man. Others described the way he would check himself when being carried away by a subject. He wrote to Friends, when preparing a reply to the priests, 'If any with you be moved to answer it, let me know and I shall forbear to put forth that which I write'.

His opponents, defending a concept of an avenging God on high, had preached a doctrine of original sin being the state natural to man, only to be exorcised by repentance and the discipline of the church. Perfection was a goal hopefully to be attained after the Day of Judgment. Friends, for the first few years of their liberated outlook, knew a freedom and joy which could scarcely have warned them of certain dangers inherent in their confidence. At the time of the Quakers' emergence as a movement, the Ranters had become prominent among the innumerable sects contending and flourishing under war conditions. It was their view of an all-permissive God identified with their own spirits which, while allowing them any form of licence as long as it could be promoted as divine guidance, often became a tool in the hands of the Quakers' critics, who could point to a similarity of structure without acknowledging the safeguards built into it by Friends. Fox had actually won some of his own converts from those among the Ranters who had accepted his precepts as truth. For him, such was his overriding belief in himself and his message, there was unlikely to be a pitfall in these people's previous experiences. For James danger was lurking both in his own more accommodating approach to others and the notable success of his eloquence in the coming months, sweeping him on as it did to a place parallel with Fox's in Friends' esteem.

In the meantime he was enjoying a fulfilment as complete as it was sudden. He could have looked back on the months of his country retirement and scarcely have believed that this influential magnetic speaker pulling in the crowds wherever he went was the same person who had followed the plough in solitude and suspension of authority, relieved of military demands. It was likely that James, in the present turn of his fortunes, might have seen his own character as having reached its high-water-mark.

There is much in life beyond the understanding of a man accepting victory and not yet knowing the achievement that lies beyond defeat. Yet, amid the applause and sense of gathering power, he was still conscious of a world outside Quakerism and its meetings, for his years of travel had taught him about the size and menace of that world. 'My spirit hath been much troubled' he wrote. 'I stand only by faith.' To judge by the records of George Fox his progress was one long tally of unanswerable assertions, each with a counterfoil of divine approval and a final reckoning presented to the offender: 'The Lord cut him off soon after.' George was in the battlefield to win; he had what we might call a Churchillian disregard for the possibility of defeat and for the inconvenience of others.

What kind of world was this strange territory of the Commonwealth that lay like a half-fabricated spell over the recognizable path of history? Less than a decade in length, its legend has far outstripped its reality, for underneath the still lingering atmosphere of civil war, the uneasiness of parliaments testing their ability to rule, the imposition of austerity and the religious challenges that resonated all over the land, there was a basic sweet obstinacy of normal life husbanding its strength. In that very year of 1653, when Nayler was released from Appleby Jail in April, in the following month an ironmonger named Izaak Walton published *The Compleat Angler*, describing his leisurely journey downriver from Ware to Tottenham High Cross, with many an artless digression as milkmaids sang Marlowe's verses to him and he reflected on life's mercies in freeing him from the stone, the gout, and toothache. At the same time, in the quiet of her country retreat at Chicksands, that grave beauty Dorothy Osborne, daughter of the last Royalist defender of Castle Cornet in Guernsey, was at pains to hide her correspondence with her parliamentarian lover William Temple from a too-importunate brother. Her enchanting letters carry no flavour of a Puritan setting. While all England is astir over Cromwell's dissolution of the Long Parliament, after a brief comment or two she returns to the subject of the orange-flower-water she has commissioned Temple to buy for her from 'The Flower Pott above the Exchange'. In such detail we may picture the relative importance of human interests in that age of kaleidoscopic loyalties.

So great was the excitement generated in the north of England by James' emergence as a leading activist for Friends that he was in danger of finding no time for sleep. Those who needed help and advice soon discovered that on top of a demanding schedule of journeys and debates he was available at any hour of the night for consultation. Time left over was given to the writing of tracts in answer to the verbal fencing kept up by the hard-pressed priests. He was often begged to stay in a local Friends' house after a meeting, but for the most part his base was made at Rampshaw Hall with the recently converted Anthony Pearson. The cost to his nervous system was mounting as he wrote: 'The work is great and a burden there is upon me.' As the speakers travelled farther afield the opposition was stronger and reactions harder to handle.

In Chesterfield they arrived in the midst of an inflammatory situation centred on an arranged bull-baiting. James, on learning that the vicar, John Billingsley, was countenancing this event, attacked him with such force that Billingsley countered with a challenge for the two to meet in a so-called 'Christian Conference'. As he was said to have added that the Quaker ought be be hanged for the insult, he evidently thought he had a good case; but the long debate that followed left James confident that he had won the day. A suspicion can hardly be avoided that Quaker stamina in wearing out an argument was a strong factor in their claims to victory.

It was becoming clear that the success of the northern campaign, with meetings being established wherever people flocked to hear the latest gifted speaker, was leaving vast stretches of the map, including some of England's major cities, untouched by Quaker influence. The year 1654, historic for Friends, marked their first organized advance on the south. These spiritual explorers had little practical support on their journeys, but for the fact that they seldom travelled singly. An opponent scoffed at 'the Morris dancers from the north, by two and two, two and two'. They needed the company, and it was an incidental boon that lasting friendships were formed in this way: Burrough and Howgill, Camm and Audland, Stubbs and Caton – names that resound together in the annals. It is noticeable that the two who were then called 'the chief Quakers', Fox and Nayler, remained unattached in spite of each of them attracting devotion from the people around him. They were relatively seldom together, though when they did support each other in the early years it was with mutual warmth and appreciation. A striking instance was set down in George's *Journal*:

James Nayler met me in Derbyshire where 7 or 8 priests had challenged him to a dispute, and I had a travail in my spirit for him, and the Lord answered me, and I was moved to bid him go on, and that God Almighty would go with him and give him the victory in his power: and so the Lord did, that all the people saw the priests was nothing and foiled: and cried 'A Nayler, a Nayler hath confuted them all'. So after he came to me again praising the Lord.

This was the only passage of unqualified support that George felt able to write for James in his recollections of those years. References to his fellow-leader were few, and one must admit that in this one the satisfaction seems to lie in the correspondence between George and his heavenly guide, without which he thought James would have laboured on his own. In the heart of this account, with its 'travail in my spirit', lies the seed of Fox's later distrust of his older and more practised partner. Why should he have doubted the success of one who had been challenged by a group of country parsons, one already known far and near for his ability to reach the conscience of strangers? Why should James have taken the trouble to seek him out when they had parted for the night, to reassure him that they agreed on victory being the Lord's? The answer must be that on both sides there was already a planted foetus of envy.

For George, accustomed to the leadership of followers he had inspired and moulded in his own fashion from the start, there must always have been a slight wariness of the man who came to him disillusioned after many battles, in sore need of a new outlet for his talents. George's love for his fellow-man was general rather than particular, subject always to his search for and triumphant discovery of divine guidance. It was the source of his strength, as well as a path of remoteness that could, though rarely, lead him astray from Christian humanity. James, for his part, was all too liable and open to individual appeal. He was by turns a winner, a loser, and a winner again in the assault of emotion. His surrender to Fox's presence could only result in love, unquestioning at first, but slowly undermined by the feeling that this evident prophet was only human, and was exercising a sway over others that he, James Nayler, knew by experience was equally available to himself. His recent five months' imprisonment had given him plenty of time to reflect, perhaps to wonder whether he had done himself justice in taking up a rôle in permanent support (for it was unlikely that there would ever be advancement) of a charismatic trail-blazer like George Fox.

Then there was Anne. Her visit 'with much freedom and great joy, beyond what I in reason could expect' had opened up, besides a response to her generosity, a flood of remembrance that belonged to the war years. How readily she had taken the load of infants' and servants' demands, the worries of work under the vagaries of seasons and weather, the sickness of animals, all in the belief that peace would see their old order restored, and that the home would have its master again. How quickly she had had to realize that men are not fashioned out of women's dreams, and that life itself is the master. She had heard about the wives of some of James' new friends; how they had often given their hearts to the new faith, had testified in ways that seemed brazen to Anne, used as she was to an unshrinking acceptance of nature. These strangely exalted young women had run naked through city streets calling people to give way to the Lord. They had suffered like their menfolk in foetid undrained holes below pavement level, had been whipped over town boundaries and exiled from their homes.

Anne was humble. She could not think herself better than these women, and yet the stubborn hobgoblin who ruled her from the centre of her household gods spoke firmly to her of her children's rights, of her husband's unspoken needs, and of her own inherited responsibilities to land and home. James, with the pull of many varied years behind him, would have realized all this. There is no evidence that he ever tried to persuade her to change her way of life, or that he resented the sturdiness of her character. The only clear witness of the Naylers' marriage being an in-depth union is the love that spoke through Anne's actions and James' acceptance, without shame or evasion, of her reappearance when all credit seemed to have forsaken him.

He was inwardly disturbed by the news that was taking first place in Quaker minds everywhere – the exodus from the north with a focal point of London. The Friends who were making this journey were men and women he had come to know well both in and around Swarthmoor and further afield; but James had continued to work alone, visiting country meetings, sometimes in answer to their special appeals. He shared the heightened sensitivity of many in that period towards the supernatural, and could not shake off a brooding sense of some unknown fate that awaited him in the capital. There would also have been the realization that short visits to Wakefield, possible while he was travelling in the north, would be far less likely to fit into the sort of schedule that was keeping leaders at full stretch in London.

The work there had been mainly in the hands of his former fellow-prisoner Howgill in partnership with the inspired nineteen-years-old Edward Burrough who had found in the older man a steadying hand without which his fire might have burned itself out even sooner than its final quenching in the Old Bailey prison at the age of twenty-eight. These two had made astonishing progress in drawing together the haphazard constituents of the London pop-ulation already interested in Quakerism before 1654. The earliest pioneering had been done by two young women, one of them being Isabel Buttery, believed to have been a member of Nayler's house-hold at Wakefield. By the summer of that momentous year the sprinkling had become a rising tide, difficult to contain unless a good-sized meeting place could be found. How this scattered ragtag of enthusiasts, led by a pair of unsophisticated zealots from the north, could have financed and organized the purchase of the *Bull and Mouth* in Aldersgate, an ancient inn large enough to contain a thousand people, we may only speculate. This achievement was in progress while Quakerism was struggling for a foothold in the city; it was to become a centre of growth until the Great Fire destroyed it in 1666.

The small groups in and around the city could hardly yet be called settled meetings, but letters referred to at least thirty of them. Burrough and Howgill, stalwarts as they were, desperately needed an authoritative figure for their temporary relief, or longer. Their thoughts naturally turned to Nayler, for surely their need must be greater than his at that moment, and they probably felt surprised that he was keeping his distance from the spearhead of the Lamb's War. This point may have been put to him with something short of tact in a letter, for there was a brief coolness between the three which has never been made clear. Howgill, no doubt personally touched because of his intimacy with James, had mentioned this in a letter to Margaret Fell, reassuring her: 'As for that which we wrote to thee of, about James' letter to us.... it is dead, and so let it pass, and whatever any judge of us, yet in the love which thinks no evil is our life.' Howgill, never one to bear a grudge, ended his letter on a very different note: 'Here is our dear brother James Nayler whom we are rejoiced to see and he us and he rejoices abundantly in his people: I hope he will stay a season here.'

For James had overcome his misgivings so far as to ride to the city in support of George Fox, who had been required to give an account of Friends' activities to the Lord Protector. Cromwell's short reign was never free of civil unrest, often associated with the Fifth Monarchists who were ready to greet Christ as King at the head of an army of saints. Because of an apparent similarity in their worship and pronouncements Friends were prone to be suspected of sharing their aim, which was victory through an armed uprising. This time Cromwell, who liked to show a friendly spirit to Fox ('If thou and I were but an hour in a day together we should be nearer one to the other') was determined to be seen to give George a fair opportunity to clear himself and his followers. It was memorably seized on in George's reply: 'My kingdom is not of this world, therefore with the carnal weapon I do not fight.' – a future tenet of Quakerism confirmed. There was something about this man that would always win James' heart, whatever the strain between them. At this stage he was still writing to his acknowledged leader 'Let me live in thy heart for ever'.

During the examination by Cromwell George was kept under guard, and James' presence was fully used by the resident Friends. There was a welcome for him in the family of Robert Dring of Moorfields, who regularly acted as host to ministering Friends. His draper's shop was one of the miniature Swarthmoors seldom given much credit but offering the scattered movement an anchorage against violence and a place for the practice of silent meetings. There was still an experimental double-frontage to Quakerism, which had to deal with large casually-drawn crowds in what were to be called 'threshing meetings', and private small gatherings of those already convinced, who understood the value that lay beyond the distractions of speech. These intervals of silent companionship had brought a saving grace into the lives of those who were so constantly challenged.

James quickly realized that his forebodings about London were justified. Friends' houses were attacked, windows broken, stones hurled at speakers, while vain efforts were made by constables to prevent fighting 'with intents to blood'. In a week or two this atmosphere changed as Cromwell's tolerance and the release of Fox became known. From being the bogey-man of orthodox Puritans Quakerism was suddenly examined as an interesting novelty. Crowds increased at the *Bull and Mouth* and Fox took on the stature of the man of the moment. He had to leave the capital before long, and as Burrough and Howgill were starting on a prolonged visit to Ireland the situation held both test and opportunity for Nayler.

For a time he flourished in it. There was a mounting elation in his reports, while others were open in their appreciation: 'James is fitted for this place, and a great love is begotten in many towards him.' It was not specified in what quarters this love was begotten, but the borderline between Quakers and Ranters was often thin, and there were many enthusiasts under both headings. Did this statement carry the seeds of future rhapsodies? The swinging climate of the city had quickly focussed on the dynamic preacher from the north whose voice had such power to charm. Nayler's attraction was often said to lie in the piquancy of a plain countrified appearance contrasting with a ready wit and engaging way of dealing with opposition. Fox, a master of invective, was uneasy about James' tactics, and questioned the wisdom of leaving him in sole charge at this critical time. He sent him a somewhat dictatorial urge to leave London and attend a meeting in Yorkshire, then to attempt to sort out a quarrel between Friends in Lincoln. James complied, suppressing a slight feeling of resentment at being used as Fox's underling.

He set off with no intention of being away a moment longer than he could help: 'I see not but I shall go with speed and back again, for I am not free of this place.' At least it gave him a chance to pay a brief visit to home and family which was becoming markedly overdue.

He tied his horse by the gate and walked up the path. The dogs were barking. No children were about. Children? They would all be girls in their teens, and the boy at school.

Anne looked out to see who approached. Yes, this time it was James. She did not fly to welcome him. Their embrace was tentative, slowly affirming. Indoors, the news they exchanged was on impulse, the realities unspoken. Her eyes were at work, summing up the latest changed man of him. Nobody reflected the passage of years with more volatility than James. She sensed a new substance about him. He wore his shabby coat with the indifference of a wealthy man who can afford to look like a beggar. There was confidence, but it seemed taut, overstretched. Of course he was tired; he had been in great demand night and day for many months, speaking, writing, travelling; and when one is always a guest, the inner nature is almost forgotten. Anne said little of her own anxieties: he had had enough of the tumult of voices.

A

LAMENTACION

(By one of *Englands* Prophets)

Over the Ruines

OF

this oppreſſed Nacion,

To be deeply layd to heart by *Parlia-*
ment and *Army*, and all ſorts of Peeple, leſt
they be ſwept away with the Beſom of De-
ſtruction, in the Day of the Lords
fierce wrath and Indignation, which
is neie at hand.

Written by the movings of the Lord in James Nayler.

AND

A WARNING

TO

the Rulers of England

Not to uſurp Dominion over the Conſcience,
nor to give forth Lawes contrary to that
in the Conſcience.

Written from the Spirit of the Lord in George Fox.

Printed for *Tho: Wayt* at his houſe in the *Pavement*
in *Tork.* 1 6 5 3.

Note the order in this co-publication: Nayler's appearing first.

40

CHAPTER V

Martha

FROM THE PERIOD of James Nayler's emergence as a leading spokesman of Friends, no more significant piece of
writing was produced than the letter he received from one of his
opponents in debate, a priest named Richard Nelson, who had
obviously felt the full power of Nayler in action and observed its
effect on his followers.

> Take good heed, he wrote, that thou steal not men's hearts away
> from God to thyself and so lord it on their conscience that they
> have neither God, nor scripture, nor any privilege of their own
> experience, but take thee as a demi-God and to make thee a
> mental idol, which is a worse kind of idolatry than all that thou
> reproves.

The letter evidently expresses something of what was in Fox's
mind when he noted in his *Journal*, on being obliged to leave James
with total responsibility for Friends' work in London, 'As I parted
from him I cast my eyes upon him, and a fear struck in me con-
cerning him'.

James obviously thought fit to keep the priest's prophetic warning among the many fan letters he was receiving; but Nelson may
have mistaken the operation of Nayler's gift on an audience for
vanity, when it was natural rather than manipulative. 'Lording it'
was not a habit of which James could ever be accused. He was rather
inclined to rein in his own eloquence to make room for others, a
fact which had been noticed with some surprise. The tragedy now
forcing itself on to his life was soon to silence the voice and benumb
the faculties that had aroused such excitement in his hearers. The

41

'idolatry' was a process created by others, sometimes out of their own needs and frustrations.

On his return from the north there was no lessening of demand on his time. Even when the numbers of Friends were increasing it was not easy to find a leader with the background knowledge to defend them as a reputable group from being accused of links with trouble-makers such as the Ranters, the Fifth Monarchists, or even the long-suspected Roman Catholics. James had already, by his relatively cultured address, attracted those described as 'great in the outward', men like the dangerously scintillating Sir Henry Vane, who brought his titled friends, partially concealed as a precaution, to meetings where they could hear some provocative views from the newly-acclaimed evangelist who was rumoured to be a star performer.

It was all very flattering to James, as is clear from one report. A man noted for his opposition to any belief in present perfection, on being told that the belief was supported by Nayler, threw up the sponge with an unanswerable yielding: 'Doth James say so? Nay then, it is truth.' It was not only the celebrity-hunters who acknowledged his influence, but genuine believers like the Baptist Rebecca Travers who heard him speak at her own church and fully expected her fellow-members to contradict him, but 'they were so far from getting the victory that she could feel his words smote them: that one or two of them confessed they were sick, and could hold it no longer'.

While she was still reflecting on this episode she was invited to a dinner which had Nayler as chief guest. The report shows her listening avidly to

> one called a gentleman, who had run through all professions, and had high Notions, and many curious questions to J.N., which he answered with great Wisdom, but not so plainly as she would have had him, because she coveted to know hidden things: on which J.N. putting his hand over the table, and taking her by the hand, said 'Feed not on knowledge, it is as truly forbidden to thee, as ever it was to Eve; it is good to look upon, but not to feed on: for who feeds on Knowledge, dies to the innocent Life': which he spoke in power, and was received by her as the Word of Truth.

This was the beginning of a friendship which was to bring solace to Nayler in the lowest depth of his solitary pain.

The build-up which had been centred on Fox for a time was now transferred to Nayler, whose meetings were thronged not merely with seekers in need of guidance, but with thrusting members of the highly articulate sects jostling each other in the city. The contrast between the two leaders was beginning to lead to complaints in some quarters about Fox's withering dismissal of any approach to the divine principle that differed from his own. Some went so far as to dub him The Quakers' Pope. The clusters of converts, who would later be quoted in bulk as 'the early Friends', contained many in whom the message was fresh and challenging, who yet looked back on their past lives from utterly different standpoints, as different as views from town and country could be in an age when these were far from beginning to merge. They had different expectations of the freedom that Fox had proclaimed for them, and while some believed he stood firm in his teaching, others were suspicious of the attempts he was devising to introduce order and responsibility into an anarchic movement. They had been regimented before, by church and state, and Fox's gubernatorial tone worried them.

James was just as capable of denouncing the opposition, but delivered his direct hits chiefly in his writings, which continued to appear hot from the press. In person he was an altogether more diplomatic, perhaps more patient, opponent, making allowances for those treading uncertainly in experienced footsteps. That was an endearing quality, but it also meant that the allowances could include voices by no means uncertain, vociferous in their partisanship. The most piercing of those voices, among a group of impressionable women for whom Nayler held all the glamour and uniqueness that in other periods would draw worshippers into the orbit of a stage celebrity, was that of Martha Simmonds, no swooning teenager but an influential Friend who could not be ignored. As the wife of one printer and publisher and sister of another, who had shared in the publication of all the Friends' writings now hawked on every street corner, she had been known to James since his first arrival in London.

She was herself a fluent speaker and writer, more inclined to project herself with the Ranters than with the Quakers who were supposed to have supported her. As one of the group openly believing that Nayler's leadership had been sent to supplant all others, particularly George Fox, Edward Burrough and Francis Howgill, when the two latter returned from Ireland to take up their earlier prominent positions, she started a campaign of disrupting their meetings with loud protests and demands for a truer authority.

Burrough condemned her and her associates with all the force at his command, describing them as 'goats rough and hairy', a comparison that few women could accept as fair exchange. Martha was a great nuisance and embarrassment to Friends, and Nayler himself at first tried to restrain her. It was at this point, brought up against a woman of rare strength of character and freshness of attack, he being eight years her senior and near exhaustion through unrelenting physical and mental effort combined with his own underlying tubercular symptoms, that his will-power collapsed with frightening suddenness. In theological terms, as he put it himself, he had lost the guidance of the holy spirit, 'and his light he withdrew and his judgment took away'.

The breakdown that had happened to him can have included two elements that seem to have been overlooked in consequent reports: sex and ill-health. Emotionally James was an average heterosexual male, having fathered a family promptly on marriage at an early age. He had then spent years separated, at an early age, from his wife. He was capable of a tenderness and charm that made a distinct appeal to women and aroused a suspicion, which he always denied, of his involvement in extra-marital affairs. The language of the day was as physical-mystical as that of the Psalms, making it hard to believe there was no trace of sex in his subjection to Martha Simmonds. Her own response was unmistakable. She adored him and could proclaim the fact in ecstatic Biblical outpourings that could pass as religious urges. They were, after all, freely used by Friends generally, even Margaret Fell being told by one of the flock 'Thou art in thy life and glory to be above all things desired after'.

The startling change in James from energy and eloquence to a nerveless silence seemed to have escaped Martha's notice as she concentrated on working the other women into a frenzy of adulation. Stung by Burrough's outburst she turned to James with a passionate plea for his support in a firm stand against Fox and his followers. At that some realization of his danger penetrated James'

44

apathy and he stood up with a desperate attempt at refusal. Martha gazed at him in unbelief, then resorted to a storm of tears that ended in a scream: 'I looked for judgment, but behold a cry!'

The effect of her histrionics, with its instinctive timing, in the words of his friend and biographer George Whitehead,

> so entered and pierced poor James Nayler that it smote him down into so much sorrow and sadness that he was much dejected in spirit and disconsolate. Fears and doubting then entered into him, that he came to be clouded in his understanding, bewildered and at a loss in his judgment.

Martha was not so far rapt in her own performance that his extremity was beyond her at that stage. She was alarmed, and having a good reserve of practical ability she took charge of the patient, dismissed the rest, and conveyed him to her own house where he lay prostrate for three days. Only a medical opinion could explain what had happened to him with such sudden and near-fatal results, but it could have been what a layman would call a stroke. When he came to in Martha's house the Friends who had gathered round were appalled at the change in him. Hardly recognizing the man who had been in the forefront of their struggles, the man many had described as 'the chief Quaker', they could only conclude that Martha had bewitched him.

He could find no relief from their attention, no interval of the quietness he needed:

> Darkness being come upon me, he wrote in retrospect, I sought a place where I might have been alone to weep and cry before the Lord, that his Face I might find, and my Condition recover... but I could not be hid. And so letting go that little of the true Light which I had yet remaining in myself, I gave up myself wholly to be led by others, whose work was then wholly to divide me from the Children of Light.

His friends felt he must be got away at all costs. Regardless of the effects of a long journey on a sick distraught person they prevailed on him to ride with them to the West Country where Fox could be found, whose influence seemed to be the only hope.

George had been in action among the scattered knots of Quakers in Cornwall when he was arrested and committed to Launceston Jail. He and two followers were kept in relative freedom, paying for themselves and their horses for nine weeks until the Assizes, when they refused to pay the fine imposed, and being imprisoned, refused further payments for their keep. The jailer, imposing his own conditions and scenting no further profit, had another weapon in reserve. The Friends were thrust into the hole called Doomsdale and left ankle-deep in undrained excrement. Impasse resulted until protests from outside, including an appeal to Cromwell, gained permission for the place to be cleaned and other conditions eased.

Throughout that summer, such were the contradictions in seventeenth century prisons, Fox had visitors of all kinds, some of them as questionable to the law as he had been, and his anxiety mounted as reports were brought in of the disruption caused in London by Nayler's adherents. He remembered the reservations he had often felt about James' effect on others. Eight months in prison, most of them in close and degrading conditions, made it hard for him to see James' apparent deification by a crowd of ranting women under the heel of the powerful Martha Simmonds as anything but a betrayal of trust. The reports seem to have omitted any suggestion of a physical breakdown caused by stress and over-work. George quite naturally felt that if he, the leader, could live through Doomsdale's worst excesses without losing his self-control, surely Nayler, a free man, comfortably housed and made much of not only by the women but by court and society folk, could keep his head and remember what George had told him many times, that the Lord's power was over all.

George was bitter. He was told that rumours were spreading throughout the land of doubt and division among his diligently guided groups of converts. He was powerless to act for himself, even with the help of the devoted Ann Downer, an educated Friend who had travelled on foot over two hundred miles from London to take dictation from him and see to its circulation.

The small procession that accompanied James as he left the scene of his late triumphs may have expected some signs of his old energy returning as he thought of a reunion with Fox. But the poison instilled by Martha had gone deep, and though Friends claimed to have 'plucked him away' from her, they were outnumbered by some of her initiates who surrounded the silent man with songs and homilies all pointing to the power awaiting him. Their opponents had hoped, when they broke their journey at Bristol, that the large Quaker contingent in what was then England's second city, would seize the chance of hearing a popular speaker and would tempt Nayler to respond. He gave no sign of interest, no greeting to any of the Friends assembling in the city.

Surely if a perverse fate had not already been felt to be at work in his life, from this moment onward it had become ominously clear. For as the Bristol Quakers began to react to his shattered look and total withdrawal, a shrill voice hailed him from the edge of the crowd. Martha Simmonds, who had broken free from the efforts made to keep her in London, had made her way in pursuit of the travellers and now, with three of her supporters, forced a way through the press of people and fell on her knees in front of Nayler with chanting and exhortation. The astonishment of Friends who had expected one of James' invigorating appearances can be imagined as they tried to recognize the speechless figure who seemed to be beyond consciousness of either their sympathy or her praise. They managed to act promptly and effectively, some pulling the apparent madwoman to her feet while others, seeing he was obviously ill, guided him to a known Friend's house. Martha was not to be so easily disposed of. She was free in a moment, and hurled herself after the protecting group, who dealt summarily with her and her followers. From her own description, 'they used us very sorely and threw me downstairs'. She added a telling note of James' distress: 'J.N. did sweat exceedingly.'

Perhaps with some intent of '*reculer pour mieux sauter*', she decided that Bristol was not her scene, and turned back towards London. James, finding himself once more in the helpful company of Friends, some of them his oldest associates, seemed to have made a partial recovery. He listened to their anxious pleading that he should see and talk with Fox – an attempt to clear the air that George himself had urged in a letter. Two reliable Friends were willing to go with him, John Bolton the London goldsmith who knew James, and a local Friend who could act as guide. For some distance, out of their concern for him, Howgill and Audland, his Yorkshire familiars, went too, and Howgill wrote to Burrough with satisfaction about the defeat of Martha's party, 'They were disappointed whatever they intended'. Her attack on those two still rankled. Of James himself he added, leaving much to be read between the lines, 'He said little, but he did one while weep exceedingly, so we returned and they rode on. We were glad that he went'.

It was a long and always hazardous journey across the breadth of Somerset and Devon to Launceston just across the border of Cornwall. Hazardous because suspicion of Quaker travellers had increased so markedly that the odds were against any of them getting to their destination without finding themselves deflected to the nearest town jail. Fox's long imprisonment had magnetised Friends from all parts to seek him out. This was enough to set country constables on the alert. To capture a Millenarian – the vogue word for anyone who could be accused, as Quakers often were, of preparing a violent reception for Christ's return – might be a speedy means of promotion. So it came about that large numbers of Friends, some of them quite unconnected with Nayler's situation, were being stalked and haled off to crowded cells at Exeter. James and his two companions actually had a pass from Major-General Desborough, the regional commander who was not unsympathetic to Friends. They were within fifteen miles of Launceston, at Okehampton on the northern edge of Dartmoor, when an officious Mayor had them arrested as vagrants and sent under guard to Exeter.

According to John Bolton, writing after their arrival, James' state of mind during their pilgrimage, despite the Bristol Friends' victory for sanity, had appeared on the surface as silent despair. The looming confrontation with Fox, whose letters had roundly condemned him and his egregious admirers, had brought his old loyalties to life accompanied by a conviction that George's censure was unjust. Much had been owed by the first leader to James' distinction of style, approachable manner, and ease of writing and speaking. James had given himself freely to the movement and had admitted George's stronger presence, his evident direct line to God. But then James could remember his own revelation, the voice of the creator calling him to service. Why should not Martha Simmonds, seeing his capacity, be equally led by God to know where the leadership lay?

The Simmonds group, at one initially with her husband the influential Thomas Simmonds, had been strongly affected by prophetic voices demanding a Sign that would prepare the world for the Redeemer's second coming. To Martha, with her apocalyptic fervour and high tide of hero-worship, there could be no figure more Christlike than James Nayler. She and her most prominent supporter, the homely Hannah Stranger, a woman well-respected in other contexts, had cherished an alleged description of Jesus by the Roman Publius Lentulus which prompted comparisons with Nayler's hair, beard and features, all suggesting 'the picture usually drawn for our Saviour'. This was to be used later as evidence when the accusation was made that he deliberately cultivated the likeness. It was enough to start the women dramatising James as the living embodiment of the much-discussed Sign, until they began to see him dangerously identified with Christ. The fact that in proportion, as their adoration increased in noise and hysteria, his customary style and presence were diminishing daily into confusion and despair seemed to have escaped them. Martha, among her other accomplishments, was an experienced nurse, yet it never occurred to her that the turn of events, propelled by herself, had almost destroyed his will to resist. She was undermining the very inspiration she had intended to create.

It may be that James, who had readily agreed to go and see Fox, was finding himself less willing as the encounter drew nearer. He could not argue with an armed force of constables, and with one on either side of his horse he may have felt relieved that George's heavy guns were being left in the rear. In vain did his two companions plead their pass from Desborough. James rode through the gates of Exeter with his mind darker than the broad hat pulled over his brow. He was a lost leader, wrenched out of his way by a contrary God whose spirit could be claimed by opposing factions. Both he and George had been assailed by messages from all the centres that had seemed bright with hope for the Quakers: from a deeply distressed Margaret Fell, from an incredulous William Dewsbury, from Wales, from Ireland, and above all from London, where the fires of rebellion kindled by Martha and her followers were still smouldering.

Friends in the capital were mortally divided. Some stoutly maintained, remembering the impact of those who had first won their allegiance, 'I am of Francis' or 'I am of Edward', while others, crying 'I am of James', could not be silenced. It was the first setback that George Fox had received, at a time when he could do little to resolve it. James, now equally a prisoner, weakened by illness, deserted by both sides of the contest, at last had time to realize the full extent of the damage. It was brought home to him that George's vituperation, understandable as it was, stood alone. It was far outweighed by the general mood of Friends which was not of wrath, but of sadness. The memory of those who had known him came back with haunting power, and not only from Quakers. He was wearing threads spun by Anne from the coats of their own sheep weathered in the winds of the West Riding. The sound of her voice blended with the words of Richard Farnsworth, the irrepressible challenger who had gone with him on their first journey to Swarthmoor, now tolling the deepest knell of regret:

'My dear J.N. is as one who is not.'

Martha Simmonds with James Nayler.

CHAPTER VI

A Sign

EXETER JAIL WAS already housing twenty-six travelling Quakers who had to share the space with its regular inmates. Whether James was given preferential treatment is not known, but it was a help that he found the jailer could accept ten shillings a week for a section that gave him some privacy, in company with a congenial Friend from the north, Thomas Rawlinson. A manager of Judge Fell's ironworks, he was later to be one of the prominent Quakers offering to substitute themselves, 'body for body', in the hope of saving those near to death who had lain long in prison.

His Exeter experience was to teach him the cost of such an offer. He and James were lying 'in a little straw, in the place where pirates lie'. From him came a sympathetic report of his cell-mate: 'James Nayler is here with me, standing in the will of God, waiting in his own way, for he is precious and dear with God and is willing to bear reproach.' Clearly James was already taking responsibility for his own passivity; at no time did he try to put the blame on others for the trouble they had caused. His mind was responding. He was distressed for the many Friends who had lost his guidance since Martha's irruption.

If at that time he could have been quietly cared for – ideally if he could have returned home – restoration would have come by nature. Unfortunately he was following a course which would have looked like a helpful refuge in the past. Fasting had often been his way of restoring balance. This time he was in no fit condition to go without food, and the fast he undertook was dangerous. Rawlinson wrote to Margaret Fell:

He ate no bread but one little bit, for a whole month, and there was about a fortnight when I came to him he took no manner of food, but some days a pint of white wine, and some days a gill sprinkled with water.

The Swarthmoor family was certainly not short of descriptions of Nayler's condition, which was discussed up and down the land in letters between Friends speculating on what had actually happened to cause the division. No-one was more accustomed to fervent biblical language than this devoted missionary household, and Margaret herself may well have wondered what all the fuss was about. Her subjection to George Fox was as passionate as any of Martha's declarations to Nayler. She was not surprised when Rawlinson assured her of James' innocence and begged her not to believe all the contradictory reports. What really shocked her was not people's behaviour in London – she no doubt had a true provincial's suspicion of what went on down there – but the presumption of a party of Quakers, and of James himself, in questioning the divine right of George to be their leader.

Martha, who seems in her way to have been a perverted edition of Margaret Fell, was also dividing her allegiance between her current idol and her husband and family. Thomas Simmonds, like Judge Fell, was able to exert a presence among the Quakers without going the whole way. She, to keep him sweet, had gone home from Bristol and sorted out her family's concerns, but was worried about James being in prison, subject to influences powerfully projected from Launceston. She must get him out of Exeter.

With no certain plan of action she set off for the south-west, and thought herself providentially led when she passed the home of Major-General Desborough and learned that his wife was seriously ill. Martha had known Madam Ann, a sister of Oliver Cromwell, and now offered her nursing experience to help the family. She devoted night and day to the invalid, who so much improved that Martha was awarded a paper requesting Cromwell's order of release for the prisoners at Exeter. Flourishing this, she rejoined her small party en route for the city, but the temptation to show George Fox the evidence of her latest triumph was too strong. She changed course for Launceston.

At best George's prison was as degrading as any in England; at worst a cottager's pig would have been better housed. That it had

had no outward effect on his stamina after eight months of it was due to his sensible care for the Lord's provision of a large healthy physique; but even for George there was a peak moment of stress which was reached when the flamboyant figure of this tormenter of his trusted London deputies, sent as he believed by the deluded Nayler, invaded his cell singing, waving a paper, and taunting him with demands for his resignation.

'Your heart is rotten!' cried Martha. 'Your leadership is a sham!'

The scene that followed was crucial in the destruction of any remaining warmth of friendship between Fox and Nayler. Hannah Stranger, close behind Martha, told him she had come down from London where she had stopped Francis Howgill's mouth. Fox, outraged, called the women devils. Hannah defied him with 'If we are devils, make us to tremble'. They then swept out of the jail and around the town, confusing the crowds who had been sympathetic to Fox, and complaining about his domination.

James, left alone with the kindly persuasion of Thomas Rawlinson, was innocent of the further trouble brewing. Intent on his fast, making a genuine effort to regain the spirit of prayer and submission to the guidance of God that had seemed to forsake him, he was equally distant from clamours of adulation and from the attempts of Friends to sympathise. In vain Margaret Fell wrote urging him to confide in her. He knew where her allegiance lay, and Fox had sent him nothing but thundering reproaches. In the wake of the women's departure came one of the bitterest letters:

James! Thou must bear thy own burden, and thy companies with thee, whose iniquity doth increase and by thee is not cried against... Martha Simmonds which is called thy mother, she bid me bow down, and said I was lord and king, and that my heart was rotten, and she said she denied that which was head in me... Many did not expect that thou would have been an encourager of such as do cry against the power and life of truth.

The women had succeeded in wounding Fox in spite of his apparently invulnerable spirit. The pain shows in his letter. It was an immediate reaction, too sharp to admit any attempt to discover the root causes of Nayler's condition.

James was equally stung. His reply to Margaret Fell, unwise when directed to that quarter, accused George of burying the name of Nayler in order to raise his own. Words had been written by this time that were unlikely to be forgotten. James' frame of mind remains beyond analysis as centuries go by, placing it further out of our reach. He must have known that he had been worshipped by a group led by one condemned as a lunatic by his most valued familiars, and that the actions of that group had destroyed the relationship that a few short years before had inspired him to a revolutionary change of life. A numbness would have closed over his brain while letters continued to arrive from London hailing him as 'King of Israel and son of the Most High', 'Son of God', and 'the fairest of ten thousand'.

These styles of greeting are less rapturous when seen as in tune with the general expectation of an imminent millennium when Christ would descend in glory. Friends and others used equally transfigurative language to those seen as prophets, including George Fox. When concentrated on the exaltation of Nayler, it was hardly surprising that he felt George was taking his monopoly of power for granted.

It was at this stage that Martha and her followers bore down on the Exeter prisoners with the news of their promised release. Rawlinson, who had been happy to see a slight improvement in James while they had been together, quickly realized the strength of Martha's influence, and agreed with the sensitive account of Richard Hubberthorne who was visiting them:

> J.N. his condition is pretty low and tender and dear, and tender love from my soul flowed forth to him... but there came Martha Simmonds when I was there and when at any time we were together she would have called him away and he was so much subject to her.

Hubberthorne, a small man with a reconciling heart, was to do all that a friend could do to soften the rising conflict between Fox and Nayler, but he obviously saw that when James' state of 'lowness' was confronted by Martha's loud hosannas and sacrificial energy a friend's moderation could scarcely be heard. At that time her sexual drive, her youth at scarcely thirty, her health and vivacity were all at their peak, captured and held by the suffering man.

As if fate's manipulation had not been exhausted, another incident arose which was to strike the balance in Martha's direction.

A girl among the prisoners, Dorcas Erbury, daughter of a noted Anglican vicar claimed as a Quaker convert, was overcome by the foul air and rigours of a crowded cell, and collapsed with no visible sign of life. God's agent was thought to be at hand: James Nayler. They hurried him to the crumpled body. The scriptural image took shape in his mind. He placed his hands on her head, saying 'Dorcas, arise'. It was a test of faith. The girl's hand moved; the body jerked into motion. It got to its feet. The women burst into ecstatic singing. The prison doors had been opened. The age of miracles had returned. Such was the height of jubilation when word was brought that George Fox, released from Launceston, had arrived in Exeter and had issued an order for James to come to him.

Not surprisingly it was ignored. A meeting had been arranged for the Quaker prisoners the next day, and Fox attended. An emaciated, unkempt James Nayler came in, supported by Martha Simmonds. The sight was too much for Fox, who launched into the flood of condemnation he had nursed on the journey. There was no response, and after an interval Fox, more controlled, uttered a vocal prayer. Nayler and his male supporters failed to remove their hats according to Quaker custom, and left the meeting before it was due to end. The reactions of both Fox and Nayler after this travesty of a Friends' meeting are not hard to imagine.

James, if he could have had the advantage of a little solitude during that week, would have condemned the burning indignation he had felt during Fox's initial outburst. The last chance of being reconciled to the man who had so memorably brought a new meaning into his life seemed to have had a fatal blow. It never came naturally to James to harbour a grievance. That spell-binding evening in Roper's parlour came back to him, the flash of George's piercing eyes and the range of his unanswerable faith. Harbouring grievances was not much in Fox's disposition either. He believed in instant attack, with victory for the Lord whether it was asked for or not. At the first opportunity he strode into the prison and made for Nayler's cell.

Hubberthorne had been working in the intervening week to bring the two men together, but their contacts had been cursory and abortive, sometimes in public places – the castle yard, the inn where George was lodging, out in the street, within the castle gates, or inside the prison: they read like a synopsis of scenes in a play, with the drama mounting as great or lesser characters move to and fro. Nayler was supposed to be in prison, the reader observes. It might have been that the pending order of release being known, but awaiting confirmation by Cromwell, gave the captives a measure of freedom, but all the time it was the two leaders' emotional states that blocked the way to understanding.

George's resentment at what he saw as James' disloyalty was too strong to be governed by the attempts he made, as he said, 'to set a pattern of patience'. One sees the impatience dammed up behind the words. James would not allow criticism of the women – 'filthy spirits' as Hubberthorne called them – to be uttered behind their backs. If it had to be said, they must hear. There had been some plain speaking between Richard and Martha, but Richard's affection for James had been such that he could say nothing more condemnatory to him than to remind him of 'whom he now was subject to and whom he rejected'. This was a clear vote for George Fox's leadership. The encounter in the street was not recorded, but had ended by Nayler calling after Fox 'Take heed of lying and false accusings!' It was a touch of hysteria which he afterwards regretted, as anyone passing could have heard it. George had challenged him about this, and demanded to know why James had not answered when he had called. James, close to tears, had told Hubberthorne 'When he sent to me there was a love in me that would have carried me through fire and water to him'. He had thought it better to retreat than to face the 'strife and contention' that would have followed.

When George went into the cells he found James sitting on a lower level than the other prisoners. There was evidently no barrier between them. When he realized that George had actually come to see him James took an apple from the bench at his side and said 'If I have found favour in thy sight, receive it'. Warily, George brushed it aside, and James, taking his hand, asked if he might kiss him – a customary greeting which, in the circumstances, he felt diffident about offering. George, still on the higher level, offered him his other hand to kiss. To James this was an imperious gesture, as in fact it was. As he repelled it, George, to make the issue plainer, thrust a foot forward telling him he could kiss that.

More than one account has come down to us of this fateful moment, including one from George himself. It was clear that he was requiring total subjection. He had been enduring the harshest sentence of his defiant career, lying helpless while news came in of Nayler's conspicuous success with leading figures in London praising and building him up as 'the great Quaker' who was their principal writer. It was too much to ask George to take – he, the 'father' of the movement. It seemed to him that it was all James' fault that his beloved structure of Friends had been threatened. The build-up of Ranterish attacks on his loyal deputies Burrough and Howgill and the ascendancy of the detested Martha Simmonds loomed large in his mind. He seemed scarcely to have noticed that these events had been synonymous with the collapse of an exhausted and over-strained James Nayler. George with all his abundant powers did not hold the key to sympathy with human failure. If a man had slipped up and forgotten what George had taught him, he must be sharply reminded. If he later saw the light and returned to the fold, well and good. If not, leave him to the Lord's judgment, which appeared to be severe.

James' was a case for forbearing love. If George had loved James as so many supporting Friends did, they would have found a common bond. As it was, he saw the offered kiss as the culmination of treachery. With a final uncompromising rejection he turned and went away.

James had little chance of brooding over Fox's action. The women and their considerable band of followers closed around him and made great play with their insistence on the need for a Sign. Dorcas Erbury's pitiful devotion was intensified as she insisted that Christ had been present in Nayler's form and had raised her from the dead. Hannah Stranger's husband had written to him 'Thy name shall be no more James Nayler, but Jesus'. Even in his confusion James had scented danger in this, and wrote later 'a fear struck me when I first saw it, and so I put it in my pocket, close, not intending any should see it'. A step taken in caution, this proved damning evidence soon enough when his pockets were searched. But at the moment when his mind whirled between the shattering of friendship and the chorus of acclamation it was Martha's intensity that prevailed. He must answer the public and private clamour for a Sign. He must appear as the living enactment of Christ's triumphal entry.

What exactly Martha, no visionary saint and no fool either, thought she was doing is hard to determine. She was exhilarated by her own power to sway others; she had openly declared war on George Fox; she loved Nayler in her own fashion, which allowed her to deify him in any way that presented itself and justify her worship in the world's view. The last possibility that occurred to her was that James, as his mind began to clear, would see himself as a powerless victim. He was to tell his judges 'I was set up as a sign to summon this nation and to convince them of Christ's coming'. 'Set up' conjures a picture of a straw-filled dummy used as a target for attack, and this is what the Simmonds party was making during these weeks of what was left of their dynamic leader. In all the incidents of that time centred on images of the Second Coming, the same defence was heard: the performance was undertaken in good faith, but against the actor's will.

When the official order of release was received, with the Protector's signature, Martha had already hired the horse she required to focus on the central figure of her charade. She needed no extra properties or costumes. In her eyes the resemblance of Nayler to the published Roman description of Jesus was so complete that she had emphasised it to Hannah and the others until they actually believed some alchemy had been at work to evoke the presence of Christ.

Towards the end of October 1656 the small procession that passed through the gates of Exeter appeared to be carrying a message of joy and revelation. The marchers sang, they cried hosannas, they laid branches on the cobbled roadway. But the silent figure mounted at their head made no acknowledgment. Those who wanted to point to the Christlike features had no co-operation. The head drooped, the broad hat was pulled low over his brows, the reins hung loosely from his hands as one of the men guided his horse. He appeared to be mutely resisting a dream of action.

They were bound for Bristol, with no direct route. The silted country lanes must have doubled the actual distance. The main towns provided some nightly lodgings, the last of which was at Chew Stoke, by which time the rain which had fallen steadily during their journey had become a torrent. They were in that state of saturation that seems almost tolerable, being past resistance. The Rev. Deacon, always bending an eagle eye on Quakers, spares us no detail: 'They received it at their necks and vented it at their hose and breeches.' In the women's case, as they insisted on walking through fluid mud, they were dragging almost unrecognizable draperies. Their stubborn determination has to be acknowledged, for the mood in which they had set out from Exeter was never affected by the dismal conditions, never relaxed into silent endurance. They came to Bristol's Redcliff Gate crying 'Holy! Holy! Holy!' and peeling off their sodden cloaks to lay them in the horseman's path.

James rode in frozen passivity. The one thought that penetrated his mask of indifference was a realization that almost unnerved him: the crowds that gathered along the street towards the High Cross were composed of strangers, staring blankly at the bizarre procession. Since the earliest Quaker presence in Bristol opposition had given way to a wary acceptance, and there were now over a thousand known Quakers in the city. A substantial number of these had welcomed Nayler when he arrived from London in the late summer. Expecting to hear a leading speech from him, they had shown warm sympathy with his illness, had rightly judged the trend of Martha's delusions, and had given him protection in decisive terms. There was something sinister about their absence now.

Silence greeted the songs and hosannas of the marching group. Not one friendly figure had turned out to support the man who had gained and represented so many ardent fighters in the Lamb's War. His own struggle to find an independent truth had only just begun. 'I found it alone, being forsaken' was to be his final witness. For James a bitter test of his latent spiritual strength was still to be endured.

'Dorcas arise (see top of page 55).

CHAPTER VII

Bristol

GEORGE HAD LEFT Exeter in a white heat of fury at what he saw as Nayler's hypocrisy in offering love while he was undermining his leader's authority behind his back. Having made his contempt plain, his next thought was to lay hands on an antidote to the poison.

He had missed nothing of what went on in Quaker circles while he was in prison: James' visit to Bristol, for instance, after his strange behaviour in London. Bristol was an important centre of Friends' activity in the west. He rode as hard in that direction as concern for his horse allowed – for George's tenderness for animals surpassed the limits of his human sympathies. Having housed his mount, he borrowed another without delay and proceeded to tour all points in the city where gatherings of Friends existed. In Bedminster on the fringe he found that an Exeter Quaker had already brought news of the plan that was afoot in the jail to bring Nayler to Bristol as soon as he was released, re-enacting the scene of Christ's entry into Jerusalem.

The mixed impressions that had been left in the local groups of Nayler's striking fame and the breakdown that followed were quickly put straight by George's warning that James had proved over-susceptible to the 'filthy spirits' of London Ranters and the obvious influence of the madwoman who had been so appropriately dealt with by the sturdy Bristolians. An idolatrous masquerade was being staged, he told them, that was on its way to the city and would bring repute of witchcraft upon responsible Friends if they did not stay well out of its way. It was a capable piece of public relations on George's part. By the time Martha's ill-fated demonstration reached the city centre in a few days' time its only observers were bemused citizens who had seen some odd goings-on during Fairs weeks, but none more like open blasphemy than this.

Believing that he had made sure there would be no local support for Nayler's party Fox rode off with undiminished energy to visit centres of Friends in widely separated parts of England and Wales, checking how far the division among them had spread while he was shut away at Launceston. It was a time when he faced in himself the need, if he was to prove himself as leader, to build a firmer foundation for his vision than a mere 'movement', inspiring and brave though the early fellowship had been. His sense of direct guidance had never been shaken, but it was brought home to him that many for whom he had claimed 'convincement' had come from sects closely reflecting other rebellious urges, and that another Martha Simmonds could emerge at any time to prey upon those he was now seeing as sensitive but unreliable seedlings like James Nayler. Freedom was all very well, and had meant liberation from church control for George, but it could easily be abused. Possibly, during those solitary rides towards the close of 1656, Fox was at last taking provisional leave of the shining certainty of his youth.

Quakers were not the only section of the Bristol community to be put on guard by the current news. There were militant priests such as Ralph Farmer and John Deacon who knew all about Nayler and had taken him on many times in the pamphlet war that had been raging in recent years. His present manifestation hardly seemed to chime with the wit and reason of his writings, which, while being sparing of the outright insults hurled at the church by some of its Quaker opponents, yet put out a challenge to orthodox religion. Farmer was eager to pin the charge of blasphemy to this repeated and well-equipped adversary. He hurried to a meeting of the Bristol councillors on the evening of Nayler's entry.

They needed no encouragement to act against these disturbers of order in the streets. An escort of troops was formed, and set out as if to intercept an invading army, to the *White Hart Inn* in Broad Street, a known venue for travelling Quakers. It belonged to a prominent citizen, Dennis Hollister, who was also a Friend. His absence was noticed on this occasion, both by the troops and by the eight remaining objects of arrest. No-one appeared to be helping or supporting the travellers, who were found amid clouds of steam by the inn fireplace attempting to dry themselves. They were immediately removed and led off to custody in the city jail, to confront their examiners the following morning.

The exuberance and singing kept up on their journey were not slackened, either when they were committed to Bristol's Newgate or the next day when they appeared before a joint panel of priests and magistrates. The silent dark figure of Nayler as their focal point was all the more conspicuous, and was the first to be questioned. Spread out before the chairman, his epistolary foe the Rev. Ralph Farmer, were twenty-one letters confiscated from his pockets before he left the inn. Farmer knew there was no doubt this time who was going to win the day. The biblical raptures written by Martha, Hannah and the rest to their surrogate Messiah were enough to make a prime charge of blasphemy. The trump card, which Farmer flourished in James' face, was the condemnation by George Fox in the letter referring to 'Martha Simmonds, which is called thy mother'.

'Why did he say that?'

James was taken off his guard. He cried out in a protest that went beyond the court proceedings to the roots of his pain.

'George Fox is a liar and a firebrand of Hell! Neither I nor any with me called her so.'

Apart from this outburst his replies were as from Nayler the practised debater, often making it clear that he had never considered himself as a transfiguration of the risen Christ, but simply as a picture or sign of the Saviour's appearance which was publicly expected. The old attacks on his moral reputation, which had been seized on whenever he had had to defend himself, were being turned over again, the Rev. Deacon offering to read out a letter implying that Nayler was the father of a child born to the wife of his Wakefield neighbour Roper. The magistrates declined to hear this as immaterial to the charge, and James chose not to answer as Deacon tried to pursue the matter.

A touch of wit lightened his testimony, as when a query was raised quoting from a letter that had called him the Lamb of God, to which he retorted 'If I were not his Lamb, I should not be thus sought after to be devoured'.

When asked to comment upon the behaviour of Martha and her friends, he sensibly suggested that they that demonstrated were all of an age to answer for themselves: which, given the opportunity, they were more than willing to do. Their replies differed so basically from his that one is bound to wonder why the brunt of the blasphemy charge was not transferred to them. Each of them vehemently testified to a belief that Christ was living in the person of James Nayler. The alleged evidence of the Roman description had been brought with them as 'Proof'. Young Dorcas Erbury proclaimed with shining eyes that it was indeed Jesus, as witnessed by the others, who had brought her dead body to life. (James would have said it was so, as he was acting under guidance.) Martha, being Martha, could not confine herself to reasonable argument, and moved into the attack with Foxian vigour: it was said that she 'threshed Farmer the priest exceedingly' with little thought for the effect this might have on Nayler's chances.

Indeed that situation, and the whole sequence of events, were so open to human interpretation that it was no wonder the civic authorities, perhaps even the priests, were beginning to feel this was a thing beyond their power to judge.

In the end they commended it to the Town Clerk, who was also an MP and was then in London, asking him to lay it before Parliament with a request for its advice. At no other time in modern history could a religious issue of this kind expect to be received and debated with comparable intensity by the government of the day. During the Commonwealth a rule was accepted that no-one could enter parliamentary service who was not possessed of 'real godliness'. That in itself was an uncertain estimate, as would be proved during the sessions of what came to be known as 'The James Nayler Parliament'. Bristol magistrates were immediately informed that the House would try the alleged blasphemy case itself.

The accused, after the removal of a few waverers, were Nayler with Martha, Hannah and her husband John Stranger, and Dorcas Erbury. They were taken to Bridewell to await a decision from Parliament, and on its arrival a troop was mustered again to guard them on yet another long journey. Such a distance, with such an escort, stopping at various posting-houses, must have aroused vivid memories in James of his years as Lambert's quartermaster, negotiating billets for hundreds of soldiers and prisoners. Such thoughts may have brought a wry smile to his face in the midst of apprehension as he tried to picture what lay ahead. He had left London not only as a free man, albeit in a state of exhaustion, but one recently given the accolade of applause from those 'great in the outward' as well as the throngs gathered at the *Bull and Mouth*. He tried to tell himself that an appearance before Parliament might mean yet another opportunity to reach a different audience, but what would be the use of that when the faith that had sustained him had become a writhing mass of doubt, like the figures in mediaeval conceptions of Hell?

Fear also had an inescapable presence in his mind. The persistence of the women's jubilation could not suppress it. Blasphemy was a capital offence. He knew well that he was living in an age when men on lesser charges than the present one could be tortured or cut down alive from the gallows for further mutilation. *He* would be the criminal to be sentenced, not the women who would be looked on almost as his victims. James had never been tempted to blame them for acting according to their convictions, which by now could appear to him to have been stronger than his own. The confusion that had receded under the stimulus of the questioning in Bristol had massed its clouds again. As he expressed it in later days with an unconscious poetic gift,

> Thus was I led out from among the Children of Light, and into the world, to be a sign, where I was chased as a wandering bird gone from her nest, so was my soul daily and my body from one prison to another.

So he returned to the scene of his mounting triumphs, a prisoner mutely accepting the homage of four fanatics, who were lodged with him in the chamber reserved for examinees, in close proximity to Westminster Hall. This ancient setting with its grand hammerbeam roof, rebuilt in Richard II's reign from the foundation of William Rufus, had seen many famous trials, the most recent being the most startling, that of Charles I only seven years before. A committee of fifty-five members had been appointed to produce a full summary of the facts and history of the case before it was to be judged by Parliament. Their work, conducted in the Painted Chamber, was so thorough that one wonders why it could not have led straight through to a verdict. It **was well aired** from the start, being attended by members who came simply as audience.

The outline of Nayler's life was given, with his army service, and stress laid on his excommunication from his home church for blasphemy and suspected loose conduct with Mrs Roper. The last charge he had consistently denied, though it had dogged him in all his confrontations with the law. 'All that knew me, in the army and elsewhere, will say I was never guilty of lewdness, or so reputed. I abhor filthiness. See if any can accuse.' This was his open challenge to the Committee, though this time there was no wife at hand to support him.

Apart from his appearances before the Committee there appears to have been the same freedom within a London detention as prevailed in the county jails. Friends from various camps came and went. Hubberthorne watched the relationships between the five prisoners anxiously, observing 'That power of darkness in the women rules over him', while James still maintained that they acted 'in innocency'. His theory may have accounted for young Dorcas, who seems to have been simple and rather pathetic, but the others had responsible sophisticated backgrounds in the business or market worlds. John Stranger was a comb-maker, probably much in demand in a society where the difference of hair-styles denoted one's politics as much as one's family tradition. Each of the four was called in turn and questioned by the Committee, and the large audience no doubt drew its breath in horror at the evidence they gave of belief in Nayler as the Son of God made manifest.

'We have gotten enough out of him!' exulted Mr George Downing, a time-server who was to be one of Nayler's most gleeful accusers throughout the trial, and whose name was to be immortalised for centuries in the address of future prime ministers. If Nayler's had been the only voice to be heard at this stage it would surely have made a fairer impression. His final statement was plain and simple:

> I do abhor that any honour due to God should be given to me as I am a creature. But it pleased the Lord to set me up as a sign of the coming of the righteous one. And what has been done as I passed through these towns, I was commanded by the Lord to suffer such things to be done by me, as to the outward, as a sign, not as I am a creature.

Among his hearers was Judge Anthony Pearson, before whom James had appeared at Appleby, and who had later been one of his converts. He wrote eloquently to Margaret Fell:

James Nayler answered all the accusations with so much wisdom, meekness and clearness to the understanding of all indifferent persons, that the whole assembly (except some violent men of the Committee) were strangely astonished and satisfied with his answers'.

The report was then tidied up to be presented to the Commons in December. Nayler with his by now embarrassing entourage was returned to his temporary prison.

Conspicuous by his absence since their arrival in London was George Fox. A curtain had already dropped over his former close association with Nayler. Ironically, it was the incident of Martha's demonstration in Launceston Jail, in which James had played no part, that had brought about George's final alienation from his colleague and friend. From that time onward the chronicles produced by George of his doings, as well as his utterances in public, avoided the mention of Nayler's name whether they actually involved him or not. Even when, at a later stage, Fox on one of his rare visits to London, sent in a petition to Parliament which was ostensibly a plea for charity towards Nayler, the wording was prolix in expounding the meaning of immanence without naming the person accused. For the most part George was thoroughly immersed in setting his disturbed territory to rights, travelling ceaselessly all over the country, to Swarthmoor for a brief rest, and in the following year making a similar exhaustive tour of Scotland. When he was in Yorkshire, if he visited his and Nayler's old friend Roper, something would surely have been said between them about Nayler's trial, which Roper would no doubt have reported to Anne, his near neighbour.

While James had a temporary respite in prison, awaiting the trial's opening, letters continued to arrive both for London Friends and for the prisoners, expressing the incredulity and sorrow felt among isolated groups who remembered James in the days of his unhampered power which had touched them so directly. William Edmundson, the pioneer of Friends' work in Ireland, whose first inspiration had come through James, wrote from prison: 'How shall I be able to stand through so many temptations and trials which attend me daily, since such an one as he is fallen under temptation? And I mourned in my spirit.'

66

Also from Ireland came poignantly from an ex-soldier: 'I am pretty well in the outward, but afflicted, yea sore afflicted, with J.N. in his sufferings.' There had been practical insight in a letter from John Audland, touching on the truth of the situation: 'It may be that the two baggages, Martha and Hannah, have bewitched James, and the spirit left him, because he would not be ruled by the Georges.' Dewsbury also saw clearly, in a letter to James:

> Dominion hadst thou given thee over the unclean spirits, that put in print lies and slanders to reproach the truth of the living God.... When thou wast in this condition under the judgment of God, the tempter assaulted with violence and to thee comes Hannah S. and Martha S.... They came over thee and thy dominion taken away.... In the deceits of their hearts wrought lying wonders and with them did overcome thee.

It was at this time that another voice, of quite a different timbre, began to be heard, as emotional as any but possibly the most difficult to keep within bounds. Robert Rich was a figure so strikingly unusual among 'convinced' Friends that it could only be taken as proof of the tolerance that prevailed among them at that early stage. Had he claimed to be a Quaker in the following century he would certainly have been disowned. He *was* disowned soon afterwards, but not on account of his life-style.

Rich was a merchant of conspicuous wealth, delighting in decorative clothes and a coiffure of well-dressed cavalier love-locks. That was as far as his conformity to any known social group went. Imagine a top-flight aristocrat of the Stuart period who might have sat for a portrait by Peter Lely or Van Dyck leaping from his gilded frame in ardent defence of a shabby outcast preacher from the barbarous north, and you have an idea of the acute embarrassment Rich was to cause his well-connected family. His devotion to James Nayler dated from the time of James' appearance as a speaker drawing crowds in London. Perhaps he was one among the 'titled folk' who went to hear Nayler with Harry Vane and Lady Darcy. If so, his was no fleeting patronage. He was to show a moving selfless love for James that defied convention and cared nothing for the mortified reactions of friend or foe.

The condemnations of Fox, very naturally prompted by the hard experience that was showing him how he had nearly lost not only the leadership but the entire fabric he had built out of his early visionary charge, were not in themselves likely to bring salvation to Nayler. It was Fox's own prophetic character that would, in that long process, play its part. But the first true reflection that shone fitfully through the mist in front of the prisoner's eyes, like a storm-swayed lantern, came to him from the pity and grief of the lesser Friends. In that brief pause between one ordeal and the next, even while the women were keeping up their fantasies in front of him, a change was taking place in Nayler's disordered mind. From that moment onward it was courage, not confusion, that took control.

Robert Rich, a cavalier who might have sat for Lely or van Dyck, was devoted to James in his punishments (see page 67).

CHAPTER VIII

Purgatory

OLIVER CROMWELL WAS nearing the end of his life. Considering his short history of struggle, achievement and grudgingly achieved power, the reader must feel that by 1656 he was disillusioned and sad. The 'INSTRUMENT OF GOVERN-MENT', of which Nayler's old commander General John Lambert was the principal author, had established Cromwell as Lord Protector of the Commonwealth, in office for life, but its numerous sub-sections were already showing awkward inconsistencies. Liberty of conscience was its keynote, in spite of Cromwell's recent suppression of the Levellers at Burford Bridge, and many were to feel that Nayler's alleged offence of blasphemy outclassed the permissible range of liberty. The Ranters, Levellers and Quakers had been quick to lay themselves open to charges of abusing the freedom defended by articles of the Instrument. This freedom was the principle for which Cromwell, like Nayler, had abandoned his quiet rural life to wage a long and bitter conflict. Of his Ironsides, drawn from the class of yeomen to which both Cromwell and Nayler belonged, Carlyle wrote 'No more conclusively genuine set of fighters ever trod the soil of England'.

Another proviso from the Instrument that had a bearing on the Nayler case was the warning that members of the minority sects should be permitted their freedom to worship in their own fashion as long as they avoided acts that could be described as 'disturbances of public order'. The Quakers were notable resorters to acts of that kind, gathering crowds, abusing ministers and so on, and it was at such provocation from them that Cromwell, despite his sympathy, drew the line. Whether the acts performed by Nayler and his followers caused any threat to public peace was a debatable point.

The fact remains that the New Model Army which had won victory for Cromwell was dear to him as his own creation. He would hear at an early stage during the trial that Nayler had given nine years of his life as a respected figure in its ranks. How was it possible for him to remain silent during such a prolonged public event? There was surely some factor at work that the records have never revealed.

The Second Protectorate Parliament opened its debate on 5th December, laden with the fervour of differing religious urges, the committee's report in its hands. It was decided that no further witnesses needed to be heard: or as one member put it, 'If we vindicate not the name of Christ in this, he will vindicate himself'. Despite this evident clarity, so many voices were raised that tempers were tried and members were to despair, after eleven days and nights, of ever reaching a verdict. The Speaker himself, Sir Thomas Widdrington – who was to give generous and convivial hospitality to Samuel Pepys a year or two later – was highly nervous and ominously over-tired when sessions that normally began at first light and ended at noon were now continued until four and even later. He warned them 'Truly I am not able to sit out these long debates, forenoon and afternoon. But if it be your pleasure I shall be willing to spend my life in your service'.

Only one voice was raised in testimony to Nayler's former character. General Lord John Lambert was considered at that time to be the second man in the kingdom and the figure most likely to succeed Cromwell. It was he who, at the peak of his successful army career, had noticed Nayler's ability and had appointed him as quartermaster. After a mêlée of protestations from all sides of being required to be 'jealous of God's honour' which was held to be threatened by 'this vile wretch' who set himself up as the Messiah, Lambert, the one person present who had some first-hand knowledge of the prisoner, rose to deliver, hardly a defence since he could not condone an apparently blasphemous gesture, but words of regret and honest appraisal of his former officer:

> It is a matter of sadness to many men's hearts, and sadness also to mine, especially in regard of his relation sometime to me. He was two years my quartermaster, and a very useful person. We parted from him with great regret. He was a man of a very unblameable life and conversation, a member of a very sweet

society of an independent church. I confess I did not think the business to be of this nature, though I heard much rumour of it abroad. It is very much sorrow of my heart, and I hope nothing shall quench my zeal against it; but I would have it regular.

Soon after this it was announced that Nayler would be brought in to comment on the committee's report.

Lambert had not set eyes on him since his army days, when he had been sent home with suspected tuberculosis. He would notice that the cough still persisted, but otherwise there was little to remind him of the soldier. The basic character of the solitary field-worker seemed to have outlasted his military days and even his assurance as a speaker. He had a new simplicity and an unpretentious dignity that was to mark his conduct during the trial.

He was expected to kneel when he arrived at the bar, as a sign of respect; he declined to do so. The Quakers' objection to hat-honour was by then so well-known that, to avoid any irrelevance, a serjeant-at-arms removed his hat. The charges were read to him in order. He admitted all of them with one exception: the continuing legend of his involvement with Mrs Roper.

'It might be she kissed me', he said with a shrug. 'It was our manner. But when I found their extravagances I left them.' When asked to confirm what he was reported to have said, he was careful to reply 'I hope you have so much justice and charity as not to wrest my words'.

When Speaker Widdrington interposed with 'Why did you ride into Bristol in that manner?' Nayler told them as before 'There was never anything since I was born so much against my will and mind as this thing, to be set up as a sign in my going into these towns, for I knew that I should lay down my life for it'.

'How were you sure?'

'It was so revealed to me of my father, and I am willing to obey his will in this thing.'

He was removed to await the final decisions while the cut-and-thrust of opinions went on for nearly a fortnight. The others accused were still imprisoned with him, and kept up their fevers of adoration, which he suffered in a withdrawn state of silent tension.

The length of waiting was probably the cruellest part of his ordeal. He had not heard Lambert's decent, if reserved, assurance to the court of his proven character. Only the prejudices of zealots rang in his ears. Having seen the expressions all round him of men intent on his blood the prophecy of inescapable death had been brought very near to reality. He looked now on the worshipping group with something akin to pity. They appeared to be his only remaining friends, and though they had brought him to this crisis, they were loyal. They did not know, any more than he did, what fate awaited them. Every day of their demonstrations pointed to their guilt, yet they were able to exult in his presence with them. If there was any meaning in fellowship, freedom, guidance and endurance, he could not condemn them.

The debate, having accepted the committee's report, continued in its former strain, and after a prolonged climax when it tried to decide whether the crime was 'Blasphemy' or 'Horrid Blasphemy' (the ultimate outrage to religion), it proceeded to spend further long sessions on considering what would be a suitable punishment.

Various barbarities were solemnly considered in the light of the menace of spreading Quakerism.

'If you cut out his tongue, he may write, for he writes all their books.'

'If you cut off his right hand, he may write with his left.'

The nearest approach to enlightenment had come from the Lord President Lawrence, who answered a virulent attack on the Quakers' belief in an indwelling Christ in words that could have been used by Nayler himself:

I wonder why any man should be so amazed at this. Is not God in every horse, in every stone, in every creature? This business lies heavy upon my heart. If you hang every man that says Christ is in you the hope of glory, you will hang a good many.

Indeed it seemed that hanging would be the outcome. A vote was taken, producing 82 in favour of Nayler's death, and 96 against it. This narrow margin prompts the thought that if a death sentence had been carried out at that stage, history's verdict on the prisoner would have differed radically from the one formed at long last under the influence of his final years. From Parliament's point of view the best that could be said of him was that Martha and her friends had bewitched him. As for the Quakers, it was likely that posterity would never have questioned the finality of George Fox's silence. In any case his heavy judgment would prevail for nearly three hundred years until Friends began to understand the spirituality of Nayler's recovery.

So he was not to die – though the House decided after all that he 'was guilty of Horrid Blasphemy and was a Grand Impostor and Seducer of the people'. Having elected to show mercy rather than make a martyr of Nayler, they produced a sentence that was to exact every other variety of penance that had been mentioned in the debate. In unsparing detail they decreed:

> That James Nayler be set on the pillory, with his head in the pillory, in the Palace Yard, Westminster, during the space of two hours, between the hours of eleven and one, on Thursday next, and be whipped by the hangman through the streets, from Westminster to the Old Exchange, London: and there likewise be set on the pillory, with his head in the pillory, for the space of two hours, on Saturday next, in each place wearing a paper containing an inscription of his crimes; and that at the Old Exchange his tongue be bored through with a hot iron and that he be there also stigmatized in the forehead with the letter B; and that he be afterwards sent to Bristol and be conveyed into and through the said city on horseback, with his face backward; and there also publicly whipped the next marketday after he comes thither; and that from thence he be committed to prison in Bridewell, London, and there restrained from the society of all people, and there to labour hard, till he shall be released by Parliament; and during that time be debarred the use of pen, ink and paper, and shall have no relief but what he earns by his daily labour.

'This was their mercy, instead of taking away his life' wrote William Tomlinson, the Friend who had left a report of the trial. Considering the general abhorrence of the offence, when it came to confronting the offender with his sentence the House was reduced to a plethora of nerves.

'What shall I say to him?' quavered the Speaker. 'Shall I ask him any questions? Or if he speaks what shall I answer? Shall I barely pronounce the sentence, and make no preamble to it? I am to do nothing but by your direction: I pray you inform me!'

Little response was given to this pathetic plea, which led to further arguments: should the accused be allowed to make a statement? The members were brought up against the awkward truth that the proceedings had been unlawful, and that the Protector, after his prolonged silence, might intervene at any moment to charge them with contravening vital clauses of the Instrument of Government, a point that Nayler himself would have been justified in making.

Finally they felt there was no escape. The prisoner was brought in, and after being informed that reformation rather than death was their aim, he had to listen to the catalogue of inhumanities that awaited him. There was no pause for his reply, though he tried repeatedly to ask them what his crimes were, as he knew none. His words as he was then removed were of quiet resignation: 'God has given me a body; he will, I hope, give me a spirit to endure it. The Lord lay not these things to your charge. I shall pray that he may not.'

As the first part of his punishment was to be carried out the next morning, 18th December, it would perhaps have been more helpful to Parliament's professed design of inducing a state of remorse if the victim had been allowed a brief time, if only the one night, for reflection and prayer; but he was immediately thrust into his former prison in the company of those who were charged with him. Several voices had been raised during the hearing maintaining that he was less guilty than those who had so stridently idolised him. Now, regardless of the discussions still continuing that would decide her own fate, Martha's excesses went on with even greater fervour, orchestrating her little group in chanting and singing with her own conception of giving support to their condemned hero. Her courage must be admitted, though of the kind that shut out any views of the case differing from her own. James' thoughts, unexpressed, may be imagined during a night haunted with fragments of a past built out of self-respect, loyalty and a spirit of adventure, which all appeared likely to count for nothing as he was lashed into total humiliation.

Back in Westminster Hall, the exhausted members had one thought in their minds, to settle this argument about the Nayler masquerade once and for all. The matter of his followers had got to be dealt with in the present sitting, as this session was likely to be the last of the current parliament. Incredible as it seems, they were to be considered suitably dealt with by a short prison sentence and attendance at two moralising sermons in Westminster Abbey. What is even more surprising, they were at liberty to drape themselves beneath the pillory where Nayler stood, in further demonstration of a relationship with the crucified Christ.

Robert Rich, who had loudly demanded justice throughout the trial, was again raising his voice in the prisoner's defence, though he acted independently of Martha's group. His brother, who was a Councillor in the Court of Chancery then sitting in the Great Hall near by, found Robert's testimony increasingly embarrassing and paid some soldiers to remove him from the scene. Being deposited at the *Bull and Mouth* he quickly escaped and was back again, singing and protesting.

It was a biting cold morning as James stood, stripped to the waist, with hands and head in the pillory, for two hours. As the great clock struck one he was released and bound by the wrists to the tail of a cart, the hangman standing by with a whip of seven cords, each having a series of knots. The distance he had to go thus on foot was two and a half miles from Palace Yard to the Old Exchange. The rule of a public scourging was one lash at every kennel, or drain, of which there were three hundred and eleven along the route. At one of them the hangman missed and struck his own hand, cutting it badly. During the whole process the only words heard from the prisoner were beforehand, 'to desire the Lord to make him go through it'. The same witness, Quaker William Tomlinson, reported:

> The bayliffs that rid as the cart went along were very cruell. Some of them trodd many times on his feet with their horses, and crusht him against the cart. Thus his sorrows were increased, yet opened he not his mouth, nor doth a harsh word come out of his mouth against them that hath thus used him, but prays for them, sometimes with tears... Such effect the first day's sufferings had upon many, that were even pierced thorough therewith, and some who were strangers, who walked not with him, were stirred up to petition the Parliament.

Among the crowds that gathered along the streets there were likely to have been many who had glimpsed James in his days as a spell-binder, he of the 'delightable melody' in speech who had drawn admiring throngs only a few months earlier. He claimed later that during the ordeal he had known only peace, but besides the suffering he must have been conscious of one-time applauders seeing him, broken and bleeding, stumbling like a felon on the path to the gallows.

Proof that James still had friends among his critics came from the woman who had been his ardent convert from among the Baptists. As he reached the Old Exchange, scarcely able to stand, he was carried to the major prison of Bridewell near St Paul's, and left for more than an hour unattended in the brick-lined dug-out called 'The Hole', that was to be his lodging with scarcely a break for the most part of three years. Rebecca Travers had got leave from Parliament to be allowed to tend his wounds, since he was reported to be 'in a dangerous condition of body'. She sent back to them a graphic account of what she found:

> To my best discerning there was not a Space bigger than the Breadth of a Man's Nail free from Stripes and Blood from his Shoulders to near his Waist and his right Arm was sorely striped. His hands also were sorely hurt with the Cords, that they bled and were swelld. The Blood and Wounds of his Back did very little appear at first sight by reason of the Abundance of Dirt that covered them, till it was washed off. This I saw, coming to him above an Hour after his whipping, in all which Time none had been with him, or sent to him to look after his Wounds.

This letter was received with a scepticism that included the comment 'I would have the merchant's wife that reported it sent for and whipped'. The tenderness she had shown to the tortured figure who had been dropped with his filth-covered bleeding back uppermost on to a pallet in the dark cold cell would have been a summons back to humanity that he might have found hard to bear. James had always been easily moved to tears, and perhaps they came then as a form of release. As she washed his stripes she told him of the widespread sympathy that was prompting groups from all kinds of religion or none to join in sending petitions asking that the second part of his punishment should be cancelled, or at least postponed.

Not all members of Parliament had scoffed at her report. Lambert had asked that doctors should be sent to him; but his request was refused. In an anxious attempt to deflect any possibility of the prisoner dying before their declared object had been

76

achieved, members urged that a panel of eminent churchmen should be sent to reason with Nayler and obtain some evidence of his repentance. But the event at that stage that caused a real sense of emergency was the totally unforeseen arrival in Parliament of a letter from His Highness, as Cromwell was styled, demanding to know 'the grounds and reasons' of their proceeding in this case. Government of the country at that time depended on an uneasy balance of power between the Protector and Parliament. Oliver, though no despot, was being increasingly tempted to make decisions firmer by accepting an offer of the crown, which he realized had to come from his ministers. He would have no more actual power as king than he already had as protector, but there would be a great convenience in being seen to exercise it.

Some who had the closest knowledge of his condition believed that his present detachment from their counsels, including his silence in the Nayler debates, had been to try to move them in the direction of kingship. At all events, as yet another petition on Nayler's behalf was addressed to him personally, he could no longer ignore the fact that Parliament had broken civil law in condemning a person for a spiritual offence. Hence his letter, and the commotion it caused among members whose 'ground' was by no means certain.

Meanwhile, on Christmas Eve, the five divines who had been selected to witness abject penitence from the sufferer had stood over him in the prison cell and found reactions very different from the state they had expected. No friend of Nayler's was allowed to witness the interview; Richard Hubberthorne had applied and was refused. James, justifiably suspicious, told them he would give no answers unless a written verbatim report was kept. They reluctantly agreed, and launched into their first requirement, that he should renounce his blasphemies.

He said 'What blasphemies? Name them.'

They gave concerted vague answers.

'Would you have me recant and renounce you know not what?'

Asked if he believed there was a Jesus Christ, he told them from bitter experience that he did believe there was, for he had tasted of him.

Hubberthorne, who was let into the prison immediately after the priests' departure, wrote down the rest of the interview as described to him by Nayler.

He seeing them not contented with plain Answers, but seeking to wrest words out of him to their own Purpose, in Meekness uttered these words, How soon have you forgot the work of the Bishops, who are now found in the same, seeking to insnare the Innocent? Whereupon they rose up, and with Bitterness of Spirit, burnt all they had before written; and so left him with some bemoaning Expressions, rather discovering a prejudice of Spirit, than real Affection to the Good of his Soul.

The visiting party may well have wondered who was doing the interviewing, themselves or the accused. They must have left not only in frustration, but with incredulity that they had been listening to counter-challenges from the victim only six days earlier of a merciless flogging.

The six days, and three more, were the result of appeals from many sources, not all of them friendly, for a postponement of further tortures on grounds of humanity. The delay had lasted too long for the patience of the zealous defenders of Christianity. On 27th December the pillory was set up at the Old Exchange and Nayler, who had been guarded for an hour at the 'Black Boy' near by, was brought up by soldiers armed with halberds who locked his head and hands into the wooden framework where he stood for a further two hours. Robert Rich, a bizarre figure in this context in his lordly finery, had been active since eight in the morning, at first in Parliament making a last appeal, then at the pillory beside Nayler. Tact being never conspicuous among his virtues, he produced a paper that announced 'This is the King of the Jews' and fastened it over the prisoner's head. It was torn down and Rich was removed, but the soldiers, not without sympathy, gave him a lift back to James' side as the executioner approached.

A full description of what followed appeared in the published *Memoirs of the Life, Ministry, Trial and Sufferings of that very eminent person James Nailer, the Quakers' great apostle*, dated 1719.

He having stood till two, the Executioner took him out, and having bound his Arms with Cords to the Pillory, and having put a Cap over his Eyes, he bade him put forth his Tongue, which he freely did; and the Executioner with a red hot Iron, about the Bigness of a Quill, bored the same, and by Order from the Sheriff, held it in a small space, to the End that the Beholders might see and bear witness that the Sentence was thoroughly executed; then having took it out, and pulling the Cap off that cover'd his face, he put a Handkerchief over his Eyes, and putting his Left Hand to the back part of his Head, and taking the red-hot iron Letter in his other Hand, put it to his Forehead, till it smoak'd, all which Time James never so much as winc'd, but bore it with astonishing and Heart-melting Patience. Being unbound, he took the Executioner in his Arms, embracing and Hugging him, after which Robert Rich, thro' his ardent love, licked the Wound on his Forehead.

Rich was never to shrink from describing himself as 'the dog that licked Lazarus's sores'.

By some means unknown, the three women also had got themselves places at the foot of the pillory, their devotion making it doubly hard for James to take a judicial view of his supposed offence. There were said to have been thousands of citizens watching the scene in silence. What would normally have been, at that period, a diversion for the crowd, had subtly changed its character to match an elevation of the spirit that had taken self-control beyond its common scope.

Again James was left in freezing darkness to make what recovery he could in the face of further penalties. A week later it was reported that 'his tongue was so ill burnt that I do not perceive that he speaks yet since it was done'. In mid-January he was taken under guard once more on a journey to Bristol that he can scarcely have been strong enough to tackle. The frequent informality of justice allowed Rich to ride with him. Could it have been the merchant's wealth that was a factor in this arrangement? Or possibly his brother would have had enough of Robert's very vocal demonstrations on Nayler's behalf, and encouraged him to get out of London? It seems that after the interval of three weeks James could make himself understood, for it was during this journey that he gave his friend in confidence his only recorded account of the painful scenes with Fox in Exeter Jail – or, as Robert expressed it, 'I received it from James' own mouth, as I went with him from London to Bristol to receive his crucifixion there'.

They were to find on arrival that Fox's influence, so powerfully working against Nayler on the earlier occasion, had considerably faded as Bristol Friends remembered James' leading role among them. The spectacle intended by Parliament to be a cruel caricature of his former entry into the city now evoked only sympathy, even tears, as he was placed without a saddle on the back of a worn-out pack-horse, facing the tail, and made to ride from Lawford's Gate down the High Street to Redcliff Gate, where he was stripped, tied to the horse, and whipped through the streets to Taylor's Hall. The sentence was carried out literally in every detail, but such was the atmosphere of moderation that far less injury was inflicted, a Quaker named Jones being allowed to keep the Beadle's arm back so that the lashes fell more lightly.

Rich followed all the way, crying out 'Holy, Holy, Holy!' as the October group had done. The Bristol Bellman was present, as custom demanded, to describe the offence, but on this occasion his bell and his voice were almost silent. In fact, it was Rich himself, with his 'mermaid's head, such was the length of his hair', who attracted the most attention until he was removed by the officers for 'singing very loud'.

This stage of Nayler's punishment, designed to bring him lowest, could have passed for a second ritual enactment not unlike the first. It was perhaps the mildness of Bristol's officials, so different from London's, that brought him the first stirrings of a sense that pain and retribution, which had seemed to be all that awaited him, might one day give place to hope.

General John Lambert: 'Only one voice was raised in testimony to Nayler's former character (see page 70).

CHAPTER IX

Restoration

WHEN THE LATEST among many confused messages was brought to the farm Anne had reached the relatively quiet time in her busy life that usually set in around Christmas and New Year. Some of the warmth that was still felt by London Friends for James was continuing to reach his home in letters and visits from any travellers who came Wakefield way from the capital. She had heard from Richard Farnsworth, from William Dewsbury, from Isabel Buttery, once in service in her own household, from Robert Dring the Moorfields draper who had been host to James on his first arrival from the north, and from Rebecca Travers who had now known him in the height of his success and the depth of his suffering.

These Friends had been reluctant to say much to James' wife of the part played by Martha and her friends. Delicacy had made their reports all the more bewildering to Anne. She had heard successively about James as a popular preacher, unaccountably whisked off to Bristol and Exeter, stranded mysteriously in Exeter Jail, and amid some kind of scandal that had involved a separation from George Fox, being haled back to London to be tried by Parliament, savagely punished, and now thrown into prison in conditions that struck heavily at his chances of survival. Rebecca's concern overflowed in her letter describing his courage and his dire need of some skilled nursing care. Was it possible, she asked, for Anne to come down herself and put in a request to be allowed to take in some comforts for him? There would be a welcome and a bed for her with the Travers for as long as she felt able to stay.

Anne was tempted. The girls in their teens were growing strong and capable. She had her brothers and brother-in-law William to rely on. She began to lay aside stores that would keep well in the freezing weather: salted meat, butter, cheese, root vegetables with turnips which he particularly liked, simple remedies and strips of linen. A pannier for one side of her saddle could be filled with these to balance another with her own few necessaries. One familiar farm-hand travelled with her, leading a spare horse.

They set out in mid-winter, facing conditions that put most of the sparse wheeled traffic out of action. Phases of the moon were important: only with its help could one travel at night. As road repairs were still managed by local government, there were many abuses. Celia Fiennes, a more privileged traveller on horseback than Anne Nayler, recorded endless mishaps and dangers forty years later.

Rebecca, when she embraced the grimy hollow-eyed figure that eventually knocked at her door, thought the poor soul looked as much deserving of care as the husband she had come to help. But Anne was tough. It was as well that visiting Bridewell was no matter of following an impulse. Several weeks went by before, much restored and thoroughly on her mettle, she got leave to see James in the company of four prison governors.

On returning from Bristol he was placed under the routine that was part of his sentence. The 'hard labour' consisted of picking hemp, bundles of the rough plant being delivered to him every day for removal of the fibre from the stems. He was paid ninepence for every hundredweight of fibre, which had to be searched on delivery and again before it left the cell. This was just one of the elaborate measures taken to protect the public from a reputed villain. The double doors were equipped with triple locks, the keys of which were never to be left singly with either the steward or the porter. Fire, air and candlelight were forbidden, a small barred window by the ceiling being the only source of light, and writing materials at that stage were also banned.

As this death-in-life was to continue at Parliament's pleasure, it would hardly have been surprising if James had felt he no longer existed. Perhaps to that end he had refused food at first and could not bring himself to start on the hemp-picking that would at least provide a little money. He sent away meat, saying it made him ill: milk and what we call a bland diet were probably all that his digestion could take. There was an unseen influence at work, for

82

Cromwell was believed to have kept in touch with the state of Nayler's health, and when suitable food was provided there were signs of his improvement.

Such were the conditions when he heard the heavy locks turning at an unaccustomed time and the cell was suddenly crowded not only with the two jailers but with four governors and, in the midst of them all, straightening her garments with indignant looks after a search, a female figure: it was no dream, but Anne, his wife. He had no doubt had many dreams of such a meeting, few of them as unsatisfying as this one proved to be, but it was a wonder none the less – her real person, brought incredibly from the far north, from home, full of anxiety and checking her rising anger with glances at the impassive faces of the governors. Anger was almost equalled by a most unsuitable inclination to laugh. All this solemn parade of caution and restraint – against what? James, who hadn't even been able to deliver a lamb without averting his eyes? James whose conduct, even when working for the militant Quakers, had been noted for its courtesy? Lord Lambert had known his man when he selected him for a non-combatant job.

She didn't laugh, though. From the sight of his wrists puckered and half-healed from the friction of the ropes she could imagine the still-inflamed weals on his back, and she saw for herself the outrage of the flaring red letter B burned on his forehead. She wanted to hear him speak, so as to be sure – ? Trying to forget the duty-bound audience, they exchanged their scraps of news, the children, the storms, floods and drought. Had he received what small food-packets she'd sent in for him? His eyes told her more than it was discreet to put into words, and the good Rebecca had contacts that would fill in the gaps.

'I'll come again' she said, and the interview was over.

She hurried back to Watling Street, and in the fragrance of William Travers' tobacco warehouse, fortified by Rebecca's hot posset, she sat down to vent her fury in the document that has come down to us as the only surviving composition in her own hand. This was a petition to 'His Highness and the Council' asking in moving and practical terms for some relief to be given to James while he remained in prison, yet envisaging the prospect of his release.

She told them that:

notwithstanding all the extreme sufferings of my husband, when his body stood in need of refreshing for his recovery, yet he is cast into that called the 'Hole in Bridewell', a cold, damp-ish unsavory place, where the damp strikes up his legs like water, when he requires air and fire; kept under three keys, put in three several men's hands, that when one is present another is absent; and is not allowed so much as a candle; being in the hands of cruel and unmerciful men, who neither will suffer me, his wife, to come to him, except four governors be present, nor suffer what I carry him to come to him, who much increase his misery beyond all orders of Parliament; their preventing of your own order may be sufficient proof to you what cruel minds are in them, for though you ordered his wife's coming to him, and that they should see that he be accommodated with convenient necessaries, yet neither of these is done....

His keepers are cruel also, one especially, Win by name, who when my husband desired a little fair conduit water, because one had put a little sugar in it, he poured it into the kennel; another time he turned back a poor dish of turnips and would not let them go in, besides divers other things which I would have carried him, to preserve his life; and this is not all, but they have raised a false report of my husband, to harden your and all other men's hearts against him, saying that he starves himself, and will not eat what is carried him, when as his body is so weak that he cannot eat what is strong.... My humble request, therefore, is that you would be pleased (if he must continue longer in prison) that he may be where he may have air and fire, and be allowed candle-light, and the atten-dance and company of his own wife, or one whom she shall appoint, to supply him with convenient necessaries out of his own state, and be but under one lock.

But rather, that you would be pleased wholly to release him for his family's sake, who have not offended you... that his body may be refreshed by air and comfortable looking to, if it may be.   ANNE NAYLER

Following receipt of this appeal, a hopeful report, with reser-vations, came from the prison doctor, but the cough, 'which he formerly got in the army', had increased, he had an open wound in his leg, and the observers could not deny his weakness.

Parliament responded to Anne with an Order that she should be admitted to the cell with her 'necessaries'. She was again kept waiting for a month before prison authorities confirmed the order. There was small comfort for her in Rebecca's news that some of the ranting women carrying protests originating from Martha were in her absence busy disturbing Friends' meetings as noisily as ever. Anne told him of this when she was at last allowed entrance, but he was still influenced by gratitude for their loyalty when Fox and many others were seen to have disowned him. She at least had the satisfaction of seeing that her support was having a good effect on his health; but springtime was approaching and she knew she was needed on the farm. At the end of March she could wait no longer, and took the earliest full moon for her journey back.

There was a definite turn for the worse when James no longer felt the warmth of her presence, and Parliament again became agitated. Sir Gilbert Pickering, who had argued for mercy at the trial, warned the members 'If you care not for him so as to let him have a keeper, he will die in your hands'. Some bright soul suggested that the keeper ought to be a Quaker 'that he might not infect others with the plague'. A message from His Highness interrupted the drift of illusion with the sensible suggestion that if Nayler were as weak as reports indicated it was time that a minister should be sent to him. They compromised by appointing 'an ancient widow' named Joan Pollard to be his keeper and supplier of diet fit for a sick man, followed by a visit from a prominent churchman, who found himself locked in a debate with the invalid and stigmatised as a 'High Priest'. The sick man was not yet *in extremis*.

The widow was under a strict rule to allow no visitors, but she seems to have connived at a breach of the ink and paper prohibition, for Nayler began a correspondence with Robert Rich during the summer of 1657. The continuing friction between Friends was now marking a reaction in James' thought. He had begun to see himself as responsible for the opposition to George Fox, which would lead to a shipwreck of the movement if it were allowed to continue. He felt a growing urge to do what he could to settle the divisions.

Rich, on the other hand, represented the major stumbling-block. His love and admiration for James stood rock-solidly joined to his active resentment and bitterness against George. He had bottled up every strand of evidence that had come his way of Foxian duplicity, as he saw it. James' story told to him on the road to Exeter, particularly the incident of Fox offering James his foot to kiss, had deeply shocked him, and he considered that Fox's signature on a petition to Parliament asking for leniency towards James, at a time when he was condemning him and warning others against him, was a significant proof of George's hypocrisy.

All this, teeming in Rich's mind, now came to the surface not only in letters to James, but in every possible communication with Friends. Finding himself disowned, he refused to be silent on a subject so passionately developed. He travelled the country challenging the obscurity to which many Friends would have liked to consign the lost leader.

Arriving in Bristol where Fox also was visiting Friends, Rich boldly went to see him, and his report of that meeting was more withering in its sarcasm than any of his outright abuse. George, receiving him with a mildness that Rich found suspicious from the start, took on the role of 'an angel of light', appearing as 'one that had all knowledge, and understood all mysteries'. This his visitor saw as a performance for the benefit of others present, for as soon as they were alone together Rich, conscious of what he called his own simplicity, 'saw that God had chosen the foolish things to confound the wise'. Clearly to him Fox was revealing himself as the Star fallen from Heaven.

Rich went back to London, where obviously the disownment measure had failed to register, for he went on:

> sitting in their meetings and hearing his and their words full of knowledge and understanding of truth *without life and power*, and seeing the enmity they bare towards the innocent, confirms me that the vision I had of G.F. is true.

He made play with the convenient suitability of Fox's name being linked to the animal of proverbial evasion and cunning. 'How subtle hath George Fox been to hide himself under good smooth words' when 'in truth he can love none but those that call him Master.'

Nayler might at one stage have agreed with this last conclusion, but by now he was very conscious that his self-appointed defender was doing his cause more harm than good. He replied tenderly to Rich:

Alas dear heart, I know there is that amongst them which must be purged, and I have learned it, yet are they the people of God, and bear his testimony.... Truly my peace flows as a river, and I know nothing can take it away.... Exceeding great is my drawings towards you all, who were with me in the hour and power of darkness, that you all might drink abundantly of my joy.... I know and feel the Lord hath not forgotten thy labour of love, in that day added to all thy former testimony, wherein thou hast borne reproach.

The spirit that was to emerge clear as a spring in James' final testimony was being formed step by step in his writings from this date onwards. The suggestion is made from time to time that the thoughts given to us as his dying words were not genuinely his, but if the questioners would turn up anything he said or wrote in the two years' approach to that end they would find the same feeling expressed in words that could only be his. In spite of the dramatic changes that had made up Nayler's story, his life shows a rare homogeneity.

At the first turning-point, 'in barley-seed time', when he was ploughing a field alone, he had had the experience that he described in living phrases to his judges at Appleby, when the voice of God had directed him to leave his home and family. His account had included, without comment, a significant sentence: 'And I had a promise given in with it.' Was this the promise that had sustained him through the penalties of London and Bristol? Had it taught him to conquer resentments which could have gathered head during the long imprisonment in stark deprivation, monotony and cold? Had it enabled him to conceive joy and gladness that would 'swallow up sorrow?'

No condition have I found like to that which is low and poor he would write. For in this I have been comforted under the power and pangs of death (when like a flood my soul was compassed about therewith) and the life of submission to the will of God, is that whereby I have known many fiery darts of Satan quenched.

Gradually the writing materials that meant freedom to him were being restored, but when Joan Pollard, who was lightening his imprisonment when she could, began to let in visitors she was sharply reprimanded. The discipline became as harsh as before, and his health suffered.

The case had lain on Cromwell's conscience and was still troubling him. Later in the summer, only a month before his own death, he was told that Nayler had had a relapse and was very ill. He decided to send his secretary, William Malyn, to visit the prisoner, who received him propped up in bed with his head on a pillow. It was an abortive visit, for Malyn, though under instructions 'to see how he was, and whether he desired anything to be done to him or for him', was clearly sticking to the letter of his order and allowing no spark of warmth to convey any wrong ideas of sympathy for an unrepentant Quaker. He reported that he had found Nayler 'under a resolved sullenness, and I doubt in the height of pride'. James had travelled a long way from his early allegiance to the leadership of Cromwell, and had fully shared the disillusionment of many ex-soldiers who had seen their visions of a new world vanish in compromise and stalemate. The sadness of their mood may have been shared by the Protector in his last days. He made no further move on Nayler's behalf. Others were watching as the patient seemed to take one step forward and step back two. It was decided that a helpful move, not uncommon among the deviations of the age, would be to grant Nayler a few weeks' sick leave which he could use to travel north and receive care from home.

He appears to have been well enough to undertake the journey, and responded to freedom and comfort with enough energy to take part in Meetings, generally in Friends' houses. A young Quaker from Orton in Westmorland, George Whitehead, enlarged an acquaintance with him during those weeks which was to lead many years later to the unlikely publication in 1716 of a collection of Nayler's writings, which had been left in obscurity under the shadow of his public disgrace. Whitehead left an account of their meeting at Great Strickland when they walked in the fields together and he heard from Nayler's own lips the details of his sufferings in London. The young man played his part in awakening James to the possibility of love and reconciliation existing in many of his earlier Friends in spite of Fox's heavy disapproval.

The first lambs were in the fields; birds were mating or working hard for survival. These were images that Nayler used readily in his later writings. He had formerly been so closely wrapped in the revelation of the Quaker message that like any of Fox's followers he had found its impact too strong to admit its close relationship with all forms of matter, with the natural world as with the spiritual one. Now, so unexpectedly released into an awakening year, its birth-pangs revealed their delight to him. Clearly it was this time, surrounded by the enchantment of some of the land's choicest colours and contours after long months of rigid darkness, that stirred the harmonies of his later song of joy:

> It is in my heart to praise thee,
> O my God, let me never forget thee,
> What thou hast been to me in the night,
> By thy presence in the day of trial.

There were quieter discoveries – some of them painful – among his own people back in the Wakefield area. He had testified, whenever his past was under examination, that the call to leave his wife and children, and the struggle to answer it, had almost cost him his life. They now saw the further cost of that response, to him and themselves: a husband and father branded, flayed, disowned by his former church, weakened by fasting and isolation, his years of authority stripped away. Their ties of blood were tested harshly in such a confrontation. To the young girls, growing up with the rumours, perhaps he would be no more than a frightening stranger.

Yet amongst them stood Anne, the constant link with reality, who had stoutly maintained her role as a wife no less than as a working mother. The girls' wide eyes quickly gathered tears of recognition, of incredulity, even of pity. He was able to take them in his arms as though the blade of time had never fallen between them.

Anne Nayler drafting her petition (see pages 83 and 84).

89

CHAPTER X

Power above Pride

I T WAS AN ACT of grace, that brief release, opposed to the brutality of much of Parliament's dealing with Nayler. No restraint seems to have been exercised, and the abruptness of his return has some mystery about it. Perhaps his freedom had been questioned. Was a field arrest arranged? George Whitehead, who should have known, simply says in a pastoral letter to Friends 'On a sudden he was brought back to the city, where he waited the will of our Father, to do or suffer'.

He was said to have been in good health on his return, and was again cared for by Joan Pollard, until the keys were taken from her when she allowed one visitor too many.

This was Alexander Parker, an early convert of Fox's, who had written vividly of the impression made by Nayler in his earliest work in London: 'James is fitted for this great place, and a great love is begotten in many towards him.' Parker now seems to have had a personal urge to reclaim Nayler from his errors. A great correspondent himself, he paid no less than three visits to James in Bridewell to convince him that by writing contrite letters to Friends he could win back their esteem. The mission came a little late, for James was already devoting himself to healing the breach with Fox and had written to Margaret Fell begging her to try to soften George's attitude, 'for thou hast been a mother not willing to cast off compassion, nor part from pity'. He sent 'My love to G.F., who is dear to me in the love of God which all the subtle workings of the enemy I know shall never break'.

George, whose early witness had been entirely of the spirit, was now finding that ardour and dedication were not enough to establish Christ's kingdom on earth. It must have a policy-based

90

counting house that would control the cost (in both senses) and organize the supporters. He believed that an almost fatal threat to the survival of his careful structure could be traced to the extravagances of those who had defied him by seeking the leadership of Nayler. In his eyes, James could not be seen as a victim whose will, at a time of sickness and strain, had been undermined by others. James was the betrayer, the instigator of strife, the narrowly defeated threat to a divinely ordered destiny.

Wounds had been inflicted on both sides. Nayler maintained that he had received more hurt from friends than from foes, and the one with the sharpest weapon was undoubtedly George Fox. Most Friends, after the first shock of numbness from the news of James' collapse, trial and sentence, quickly reacted with deep sorrow and a desire to see him reinstated. They felt that the solution would lie in a public repudiation of the Martha Simmonds demonstrations. This was most tenderly expressed by William Dewsbury, who relied in his appeal on the hurt to the spirit which was threatened by the vehemence and self-will of the rebel party. Only James could do anything towards dispersing them. Make a real gesture, Dewsbury urged him, to show them he realized they had taken the wrong path.

This was no easy step for James, who was ready to take all the censure for his own actions but could not condemn the others. The reservation was implicit in his reply:

> My heart is broken this day for the offence that I have occasioned to God's truth and people, and especially to you, who in dear love followed me, seeking me in faithfulness to God.... I beseech you forgive wherein I evilly requited your love in that day.

The plea is solely on his own account. His normally clear judgment was asserting itself.

There was a similar acceptance of responsibility in the paper he sent to Parliament, which may have provided the grounds for his temporary release. Declaring his allegiance only to Christ, he testified that 'to ascribe this name, power and virtue to James Nayler (or to that which had a beginning and must return to dust) or for that to be exalted or worshipped, to me is great idolatry'.

Parliament had estimated the length of his imprisonment as being determined by its 'pleasure'. It should have felt, on reading this message, that Nayler's account had been settled, but when Oliver was succeeded by his less amenable son the climate changed. Richard Cromwell had never disguised his horror at the insult to Christ performed at Bristol, and had pronounced himself fully in favour of Nayler's execution. James had already served nine months imprisonment – three more than the time decreed for a first offence of blasphemy – but he was to remain with harsher treatment until Richard's inevitable defeat occurred and the Long Parliament was reassembled.

In September 1659 James was at last released and was warmly received by the Travers family 'at the Sign of the Three Feathers' in Watling Street. Longing above all to be reconciled to Fox, he heard that George, then in Reading, had been prostrated by a feverish illness probably caused by mental stress. Without delay James rode hopefully to see him. George's door was shut in his face. It is baffling to try to understand how George, a great spiritual leader, could flatly refuse such an approach by James whose capacity was so well known to him, who had paid for his brief weakness with such extremity of suffering and had used every means in his power to publish his repentance. A belief that George had never been able to share in the general affection for James does not make it any easier to defend his attitude to one he would naturally regard as a weaker vessel.

One wonders if Margaret Fell ever told George of the letter she received from James after that abortive visit:

I suppose thou may have heard of my going to see our beloved G.F. at Reading, which in tenderness of love I did as I got out of prison, hearing he was not well. But I was not permitted to come where he was, which my adversary rejoiced at, that thereby he might add sorrow to affliction. But my spirit was quieted, in that simplicity in which I went, in that to return; and he gave me his peace therein, as though I had had my desire

The words show James already on the way to his final expression of the spirit that salutes the good and bows sweetly but dismissively to a sense of being wronged.

As yet Fox had shown no sign of realizing that a rapprochement between himself and Nayler would be necessary before the movement could recover its strength. The reports that reached him were of welcome given to James in all the circles that had formerly enjoyed his speeches and publications, and of their renewed exercise. In a remarkably short time he was addressing overflowing meetings and helping Friends in distress. It was a time of unrest and reaction, and of bitterness in some quarters when the people's conscience, over which so much blood had been shed and victory acclaimed, seemed to have been forgotten and the return of the exiled heir of Charles I was planned and accepted.

Nayler was once again in the centre of political issues, a scene which had never failed to stimulate him in the past; but he had been profoundly altered by his recent experience. It was as if his inmost being had been hidden from view and had been newly discovered as material for reconciling human beings of opposite convictions. He went about as freely as before, but no longer to make faith a battleground among professing Christians. His message was of simplicity, patience and love. 'This is joy indeed, and love unspeakable, when the soul finds that treasure in his own house freely given, which he hath long been seeking abroad, and could never purchase, neither with life nor estate.'

Fox was back in London, noticeably avoiding meetings where James was expected, but he had to concede the persisting devotion with which William Dewsbury had been working towards an ending of the division. Dewsbury, who had been travelling among Friends in Scotland and the north of England, made a special journey to London to arrange a meeting which he prevailed upon George to attend.

No details have survived of the room where this crucial encounter took place. It must have been small, almost intimate, certainly not a 'threshing' meeting for all enquirers, but it probably included as many well-known Friends as had ever been brought together for a single event: Dewsbury, Burrough and Howgill, George Whitehead, Caton and Stubbs, Bolton, Farnsworth, Anthony Pearson, Rebecca and William Travers – and at last, Nayler and Fox.

James would have had the date among his formal invitations and would have been among the first to arrive. Silence had already settled, with a certain apprehension, when the sturdy figure of George Fox appeared and made for the chair obviously reserved for him. A further silence followed. Dewsbury held his breath. He was in the confidence of both men, and knew what had to happen. George had been adamant that there must be complete subjection in the style he had demanded at Exeter. James got up, took the step or two between himself and George, knelt down and touched the outstretched foot with his lips.

Dewsbury released his breath slowly as James remained kneeling, and an extraordinary thing happened. One by one the familiar figures knelt with him, not pointedly in subjection to Fox, but in mutual worship of their shared Lord. It was Dewsbury whose description of the scene was to reach posterity, giving such jubilant expression of his relief that perhaps he overstressed the sense of celebration:

> Mighty was the Lord's Majesty among his people in the day he healed up the breach which had been so long to the sadness of the hearts of many. The Lord clothed my dear brethren G.F., E.B., F.H., with a precious wisdom. A healing spirit did abound within them with the rest of the Lord's people there that day.

He added his own touch of tenderness: 'And dear J.N. the Lord was with him.'

But there was one witness who found the spectacle anything but exhilarating. Robert Rich, who felt bound to keep an eye on the outcome of the event, had remained in a back seat and added nothing to the silent chorus of acquiescence. Respect for the spirit of James' act had kept him silent, but long after the death of his friend his still smouldering resentment flared up in a letter to Fox, which was printed in his pamphlet 'Hidden Things Brought to Light'. From this we are able to piece together the actual course of the meeting. Rich's sense of outrage was so strong that he was even critical of James, who in his eyes was the victim rather than the beneficiary of George's concession. Recounting their Exeter meeting, he goes on:

> Moreover didst not thou G.F. and thy friends still continue your enmity towards him, so long, till for love and peace he bowed down to thee, making himself of no reputation, yea, sin, that knew none, rather than ye by continuing your enmity against him should destroy your souls whom he so much loved; and was not this, think ye, the mind of Christ Jesus in J.N. which ye call his weakness, fall and recantation? .... When G.F. offered to J.N. his hand, and afterwards his foot to kiss, whether J.N. in falling down and worshipping, had not given that honour to man which belongs to God alone; which honour the faithless

generation gives and receives one of another, and not the honour that cometh from God alone: and when James Nayler and several others went down upon their knees before G.F. to confess (as divers have reported that were eye-witnesses) and what myself have seen... is not this to worship men, which is idolatry?

With our hindsight, realizing that George only brought himself to accept Nayler's homage as a public necessity rather than the gesture of penitent love that inspired it, we know that it formed part of the leader's resolute building of an edifice that would be proof against 'notions' and backsliding – even strong enough to temper the sympathy of Margaret Fell, who could write about the historic Quaker impact at Swarthmoor Hall without even mentioning the name of James Nayler. Fox was ensuring the fall of a blanket of silence over Nayler's contribution to the genesis of Quakerism.

There was no sense of incompleteness in James' mood in the months following the 'reconciliation'. Demand for his appearances was greater than ever, and in spite of the turbulence in London streets the Quakers' Meeting-place in the Strand, where he spoke most often, needed overflow space to cope with his audience. There may have been an element of the sensational in this public demand. The wax effigy of 'James Nayler the Mad Quaker' had begun to gather its legendary character in some quarters, and after nearly three years in prison people probably wanted to know what he looked like, but the rare peace and conviction of his testimony quickly touched the hearts of even the curious. These Meetings were taxing his energies when he needed a longer interval of recovery, but the pull of natural ability was hard to resist.

Any spare time was filled with correspondence and the writing of pamphlets. The letter he sent to King Charles on his accession pleaded for the Quakers, not in his old attacking style, but in gentle and reasonable terms:

O King! God hath in these nations a people gathered by himself into his light, and though we cannot swear and unswear, covenant and uncovenant with every change that comes, as men do that know not the everlasting covenant and decree of God, yet this hath God sealed in our hearts: to seek the good of all men, plot against none: but study to live quietly, and exercise our conscience faithfully towards whatever government our God shall set up.

Not all his exhortations were as mild as this. The Friends were stirred to great concern over the cruelty to their immigrant members in New England, and Nayler's condemnation of Governor Endicott hit out powerfully in the victims' defence:

O men, be ashamed of your words! Are they not known in England to have been men who generally did adventure lives and estates?... And now seeing they cannot seek it that way, do they not sit down and suffer, in the way of Christ, all that man hath power to inflict upon them?... May not all that ever heard what you once fled from, out of England, stand amazed at this return?

When we look, not for the public champion, but for evidence of James as he was in the homes of Friends, not preaching but unobtrusively proving that his presence brought a quiet authority into the company, we have a stroke of good fortune in the emergence of a new character who could picture such a scene with the pen of a keen-eyed writer. This was young Tom Ellwood, Milton's future friend and amanuensis, to whom Nayler was virtually a stranger. James had come in support of Edward Burrough who was to speak at a Meeting near the Chalfont home of Isaac and Mary Penington, old friends of Ellwood Senior who had brought his son with him to demonstrate to the lad his own well-polished views on the troublesome Quakers.

After the Meeting the visitors were entertained to supper in the Peningtons' house, where the father soon discovered that his formerly worldly hosts had become whole-hearted Quakers, giving him ample provocation for argument. Against the Friends' theme of the free grace of God to all mankind he opposed his own theory of predestination. His volubility had begun to embarrass his son, who was finding the Quakers' views more to his liking. Let the twenty-year-old take over the story:

Edward Burrough said not much... but James Naylor interposing, handled the subject with so much perspicuity and clear demonstration, that his reasoning seemed to be irresistible; and so I suppose my father found it, which made him willing to drop the discourse. As for Edward Burrough, he was a brisk young man, of a ready tongue, and might have been, for aught

I then knew, a scholar, which made me the less to admire his way of reasoning. But what dropt from James Naylor had the greater force upon me, because he looked but like a plain simple countryman, having the appearance of a husbandman or a shepherd.

Thus at this late stage in Nayler's history we have, as an unexpected gift, a vignette that shows him to us more vividly than any of the stilted terms of Commonwealth writers. Time was taking a hand in the shaping both of thought and style that would lead rapidly to the ease and humanity of William Penn. It seems a pity that Tom did not quote some of Nayler's reasoning which had impressed him so much, but he certainly conveyed the fact that when James was forty-one his mutilated tongue could communicate with youth more appealingly than the 'ready tongue' of a speaker only seven years older than Tom himself.

There was one act of contrition that Nayler willingly undertook. He realized that many Friends in Bristol had been deeply hurt and confused by Martha Simmonds' fantasies and Nayler's mute compliance. That city had known many crises in the mid-century, not only arising from the war years. Friends had achieved a healthy and growing community after the arrival in 1654 of Camm and Audland who had triumphed on ground prepared for their message by large receptive groups of seekers. They felt that further progress was in peril from the notoriety of the Nayler scandal. Their decided action against Martha had been accompanied by an effort to help and protect him, and it was they who arranged the escort to go with him to see Fox. Fate had intervened at that point, and the 'entry' staged by Martha must have appalled the Bristol Friends, who felt that even for James' sake they could not be seen to support it. In his ultimate recovery he understood their feelings and wished to make that plain.

A written apology to the authorities, which he had sent, was not enough. Late in 1659, possibly accompanied by the ever-helpful Hubberthorne, he made his third significant appearance in Bristol before a Quaker gathering. It was perhaps all to the good that Robert Rich's voice was not heard on this occasion. He had shaken the unaccommodating dust of London off his feet and departed for his business centre in Barbados, to remain there for twenty years before a spectral reappearance in England to re-enact

97

his part in Nayler's trial and punishment and revive the memory of his hero.

Standing in the place which had precipitated his downfall James was aware that he had to win back an audience that was all too conscious of that pelting wet day only three years before. He now spoke quietly, with a depth of emotion quite outside the range of power that had held people spellbound from his years of army service. He had not then been able to draw on the scars of flesh and spirit that would teach him to say:

> Art thou in darkness? Mind it not, for if thou dost it will fill thee more; but stand still and act not, and wait in patience till light arise out of darkness to lead thee. Art thou wounded in conscience? Feed not there, but abide in the light which leads to the grace and truth, which teaches to deny and put off the weight, and removes the cause, and brings saving health to light.... And this I have learned in the deeps, and in secret, when I was alone, and now declare openly in the day of my mercy.

Several in that gathering witnessed to a reporter that hardly anyone present could refrain from tears.

If London's citizens had counted on the reign of Charles II to bring in an era of peace and tolerance there were sharper lessons in store. The unofficial sects suffered more persecution than ever, and the Quakers, who aroused most fear in government circles, had harsher treatment than any. James returned to London and took his place as the most prominent free-speaker in the City. It may be that the darkness out of which he had won his way to freedom had left him with a special affinity towards those living under such threats. In the years before his crisis he had never avoided contention, taking on the accusations of church defenders with lively cut-and-thrust, and a ready answer in print or speech to every point raised.

The concern about poverty and the underdog which had motivated him no less than his friends in Cromwell's army had given place in the end to an emphasis on the saving grace of Christ and the coming of the millennium. Isolation in a prison cell had shown him that judgment came down at last to a dialogue between the spirit of God in man and 'the creature' – that is, himself in the flesh. The conquest of weakness and fear was man's own responsibility, as Hamlet had put it, 'whilst this machine is to him'. He confronted the disillusion and speculation in the Friends who came to hear him with the voice of one who had faced the furthermost test.

Were thy afflictions as great as Job's, and thy darkness as the depths of the sea, yet if thou wilt not run to vain helps as I have done, but stay upon the Lord till he give thee light by his word, from thence will he bring thee forth, and his eye shall guide thee, and thou shalt praise his name as I do this day.

After their reconciliation Fox was travelling elsewhere, but he lost no opportunity of keeping an eye on Nayler's progress in the capital. There was still an undercurrent of wariness between them. Each knew the other's potential for use or misuse of an outstanding character. There could never be the same frankness and ease between them as had existed in their early relationship. Significantly it was Hubberthorne who was advised in a letter from Fox that it might be more useful for Nayler, instead of staying in London, to journey up to 'Bishoprick', the former name of County Durham. This was during the close and oppressive summer of 1660. The suggestion probably arose because of a concern that Anthony Pearson, notably won for the Quakers by Nayler's testimony at Appleby, had shown signs of backsliding into his inherited advantages of money and position. He had defended many hard-pressed Friends since that day, and sheltered many at Rampshaw Hall. The loss, if it proved so, would be keenly felt. Perhaps George, fighting his own battles, thought 'It was Nayler who influenced him, so let him try again'. Hubberthorne quoted his letter to James, who found it difficult to answer. He had assured George of his readiness to respond to any call from him, but this came at a moment when he was surrounded by the pressing need and appreciation of London Friends. There was some correspondence (not surviving) on this matter, Fox not accepting the explanation until James finally consented to leave his post.

Uppermost in his mind was the thought that he now had a legitimate chance of going by way of Wakefield and visiting his family. Autumn was in the air; rain had turned the dusty roads into sludge, less dramatically than the drench that had fallen on the pilgrimage to Bristol, but probably even worse underfoot. Why had James chosen to walk many long miles northward when a horse was usually available for travelling Friends? Perhaps he had thought of getting to Wakefield and finding a familiar mount from the farm?

In the months following his release he had been drawn into almost constant activity, high in emotional demand on a man of limited physical strength. The cough was still in evidence. He no doubt welcomed the fresh air and the prospect of silent thought. As he walked free of London and rested now and then by a country roadside a strange mood came over him. He could be recognized by most Friends in the area. Not far from Hertford a familiar figure appeared, expecting a warm greeting, and drawing nearer, was surprised that the seated figure neither raised a hand nor stirred. It *was* Nayler...? The arched nose under the pulled-down hat was unmistakable, but he appeared to be, as this old acquaintance tried to describe him later, 'in a very awful weighty frame of mind'. He roused himself when spoken to, but evaded the man's concern and the offer to rest at his home. He had to go on to Huntingdon, he said, and struggled to his feet, leaving the Hertford Friend gazing after him. It was not an encounter that would be quickly forgotten.

James managed to hasten his step and stir his settling blood. He was on the old Roman Ermine Street, straight as prison bars, but there were still many miles ahead before Huntingdon. He was locked in a superhuman effort to keep on his feet, a formless prayer in his head that he might be welcomed at home, changed and scarred as he was. Reaching the town, the muscle constraint never slackened and he plodded on, street after street at the same pace. His head ached and a slight shiver started through his drawn lips. There was no sun.

Once more he came to the notice of a local Friend, who wrote that he looked 'in such an awful frame, as if he had been redeemed from the earth, and a stranger on it, seeking a better country and inheritance'. 'Awful' again: this was not the James Nayler whose roots were in the land, who could so effectively combine the look of a countryman with the skill of a practised speaker. This was the look of a dedicated explorer calling on every remaining shred of his strength.

He covered a mile or two beyond the town and was forced to rest on the soft turf left at the roadside for drovers' flocks. The sleep he had battled against took its advantage. When he opened his eyes two or three unkempt figures stood over him. One of them knocked him back as he tried to rise. They pulled off his dalesman's coat. It was old and serviceable, the only thing about him that had any marketable value. A few coins were in the pockets. He reached for the coat, and while one took his hat that had lain on the grass, another tied his wrists together with breeches cords. They lifted him easily, flung him into the adjoining field and made off down a side-track before any mounted traveller could appear. It had been, as an attempted robbery, hardly worth the effort.

He was semi-conscious and hardly aware of time passing. The light was fading when a farm worker, taking a short cut homeward, came round the edge of the stubble field and caught sight of a pale shirt sleeve. The sick man lay with an arm stretched over a tussock of grass. His reply to the stranger was confused. The man took off his leather jerkin, laid it over the recumbent figure and told him he would fetch help. By a kindly chance the nearby hamlet of Holm contained a family of Quakers who came out to see who was disturbing their elderly neighbours. Father and son hurried out to the spot where James lay, and supported him to their home.

Washed and given clean linen, his identity was discovered and he, lying in the comfort of a bed, made his last conquest as he cleared his throat, drank the proffered water and was able to speak. 'You have refreshed my body', he told them, smiling. 'The Lord refresh your souls.' As his voice trailed into silence he was asleep.

He was not badly hurt, but the journey had taken what was left of his reserves. Early next morning the family called in a Friend from Kings Ripton, Dr Thomas Parnell, who saw that Nayler was dying. They formed a vigil beside him for most of that day, one or another coming and going silently with necessaries. The warmth and care revived him a little. He spoke at intervals, and a young man present who realized that James wished a message to be recorded, fetched pen, ink and paper and wrote down the halting sentences, waiting patiently between each. Seen as an unbroken narrative, the message ran:

There is a spirit which I feel that delights to do no evil, nor to revenge any wrong, but delights to endure all things, in hope to enjoy its own in the end: its hope is to outlive all wrath and contention, and to weary out all exaltation and cruelty or whatever is of a nature contrary to itself. It sees to the end of all temptations; as it bears no evil in itself so it conceives none in thoughts to any other: if it be betrayed it bears it; for its ground and spring is the mercies and forgiveness of God. Its crown is meekness, its life is everlasting life unfeigned, and takes its kingdom with intreaty and not with contention, and keeps it by lowliness of mind. In God alone it can rejoice, though none else regard it, or can own its life. It's conceived in sorrow, and brought forth without any to pity it: nor doth it murmur at grief and oppression. It never rejoyceth, but through sufferings; for with the world's joy it is murdered. I found it alone being forsaken; I have fellowship therein, with them who lived in dens, and desolate places in the earth, who through death obtained this resurrection and eternal holy life.

The friendly doctor had a small garden in Kings Ripton which he offered as James' burial place. His new-made friends stood in silent worship as he was laid in the ground. With them, unseen, were other spirits from far and near: Anne whose working life had moved in an invisible partnership with her readiness to keep faith in time of need; the soldiers who had fought or tramped at his side; Francis Howgill who had shared and talked the night through with him in a Westmorland village lock-up; impetuous Farnsworth the stimulus on their early travels; Dewsbury whose Christianity was an invisible armour to their friendship; little Richard Hubberthorne, slow of speech and fast of understanding, who had always been on hand to support and conciliate. There would have been more recent Friends: young Tom Ellwood, an instinctive interpreter of James' feeling; Robert Rich with his ungovernable love, who was overly literal in his response to the text 'Of him to whom much is given, much will be required'; and the final touch on a tortured body, the healing fingers of Rebecca Travers.

The predominant note in James' closing message is of joy. Its clarity is an appeal to humanity, that those who suffer may live to see beyond the world's notion of gain to the heart of simple living where joy can exist in silent discovery. In this spirit he had been able to write:

In the deep didst thou show me wonders
    And the forming of the World...
Then did the Heavens shower down
    And thy glory descended...
Thou filledst the lower parts of the earth with gladness,
    And the springs of the valleys were opened...
Thou madest thy plant to spring,
    And the thirsty soul became as a watered garden.

CHAPTER XI

Postscript: The Seeds of Time

AND GEORGE FOX? He was too honest a man to have joined the company by that nameless grave without a feeling of relief. His path lay ahead of him, needing fewer backward glances at its first major crisis, fewer haunting thoughts of what might have happened if Martha Simmonds had not defied him with the order of release for the Exeter prisoners.

After Nayler's sentence George was travelling among centres where Friends had multiplied, and finding for himself the real regard for Nayler that underlay the immediate shock. He was realizing that his leadership lay in the balance, and that he had to work hard to substitute reliable organization and practical support for the insubstantial appeal of the Nayler party as promoted by Simmonds. It was not enough to condemn them as Ranters. If Nayler had walked free from that time onward he would never have lacked followers. His story is dogged throughout by the small syllable 'If...' and occasionally by 'If only...' If the cloud had lifted earlier from his overstrained mind: if he had remained in the kindly restorative care of Thomas Rawlinson at Exeter instead of being subjected to the invading pressure from the women to embody their 'sign', the appearance of George at that stage could well have led to a sorting-out of resentments on both sides. 'The love that would have carried me through fire and water to him', as James expressed it, would have prevailed before it was too late.

Life expectancy was short at that period, and for suffering Friends even shorter. Most of James' familiars were gone within the decade after his death: Hubberthorne, Burrough, Howgill, Farnsworth. With the exception of Dewsbury, who was seldom out of jail long enough to keep Nayler's memory alive, and Rich who had preserved it with undiminished loyalty but was far enough away to cause no more trouble to his relatives, there was no prominent figure to raise a voice against the decree of oblivion laid down by George Fox. The distance implied in Fox's writings by James' absence was emphasised in a brief mention to a correspondent that he had been informed 'that James Nayler hath finished his course, the manner of his departure I can say little of, save that it was in the peace of God'.

Margaret Fell was extremely careful to follow George's example. Whenever she described the early achievements of Friends she translated Nayler's share as '....and another'. This deliberate smothering of a prominent figure meant that, for a time at least, it was the notoriety of his public condemnation, which could scarcely be ignored, that clung to Nayler's name instead of a balanced judgment of his life. For this injustice one is bound to see Fox as largely to blame. He may have burned with resentment and believed that all the right was on his side, but as the prophet and instigator of an affirmative movement he could not avoid responsibility for fair play towards one who had placed his whole future and his great power to inspire entirely at the disposal of Friends. The irony emerges that it has been the deeply moving quality of Nayler's spirit under this injustice that has shown clearly in the end who was the Christian instrument.

Some readers of this book may have missed the provision of notes and references that are expected to accompany lives of historical characters. It was hoped that the average reader, for whom the work was planned, would find it a pleasure to be relieved of the need to turn the page elsewhere before going on with the story. Five essential sources have been available, and as each new situation arose it has been re-considered in all of them. With the exception of the first, they deal with every detail of Nayler's history as far as it is known with scholarly attention; yet each is markedly different from the others, according to the rewards that each writer was seeking to find and convey.

The five are, in order of publication:

1. James Nayler: Works. A Collection of sundry books, epistles and papers. Ed. George Whitehead. 1716.

2. The Quakers' great treasury of biographical literature written in the early 1900's, *The Beginnings of Quakerism* by William C. Braithwaite. This inexhaustible book shows charity ahead of its time in understanding Nayler and in the amount of space given to his actions before, during and after the crisis. Macmillan 1912 and currently Sessions of York.

3. *A Quaker from Cromwell's Army: James Nayler* by Mabel Richmond Brailsford. As an introduction to the subject, this would be hard to match. Few notes are used, but the background knowledge, balanced judgment and unsentimental narration are all admirable. The Introduction is a most helpful summary of the cross-currents and convoluted faiths of that unique era of English history that led to the emergence of Quakerism. The author's comment: 'The 46 sects which were reckoned during the Commonwealth were unanimous in their love of God and their hatred of the other forty-five' is characteristic of a style that allows us to see an often deeply painful subject with detachment and humour. Swarthmore Press 1927.

4. *The Rebel Saint: James Nayler* by Emilia Fogelklou. This Swedish writer follows each step of the tragedy with close personal involvement and impressive documentary resource. Some would find her a little over-emotional, handling a subject that needs to deal warily with emotion, but her range of quotations is valuable. Ernest Benn 1931.

5. *James Nayler – the Quaker indicted by Parliament* by William G. Bittle. The sub-title shows us the author's predominant interest. It is a mine of information on Cromwell's Government and on the proportions of parliamentary divisions, as well as on details of Nayler's writings and the conduct of his opponents during the pamphlet war. Personalities are condensed, and remain to some extent lay figures. The appendix and notes occupy about a quarter of his script. The chapter on the Quaker thought of James Nayler, while admitting that its study needs to be grounded in a larger context, is a valuable aid to understanding the arguments that went on for so long between the Friends and churchmen, often consisting of answers to answers to answers, *ad infinitum*, so that the original statement is lost, one suspects, in the effort to gain points. Sessions of York 1986.

It will be seen that each of these authors throws such an individual light on the subject that they are inter-dependent and need each other to complete a picture of a many-faceted subject. Like any other writer on such a theme, I have felt constantly indebted to all these works, as well as to the successive editors of Fox's *Journal*. My own approach has been within the pull of sheer story-value, dramatic interest, the clash of characters and the build-up of tragedy with its peaceful but challenging aftermath.

No-one who reads about the establishment of Quakerism and the few short years of its astonishing spread in a country already charged with a Puritan spirit, can avoid asking why so many advantages gained in previous centuries seem to have had wholesale denial by those so zealous in the search for God's truth. Fox had no intention of forming a new sect, and had found no satisfaction in the ones that existed increasingly in the 1650's. The inward light, he told his followers, was freely available to all and needed no assistance from intermediaries such as paid ministers, governments or the law. The two latter had their place and need not be resisted, but the clergy were an encumbrance on the Lord's access to his people. They preached 'the Letter', which meant a literal application of biblical texts, against 'the Word', which was the animating spirit of Christ in his 'dear lambs'. 'The Word' said Nayler 'is quick and powerful, to the dividing asunder the joints and marrow, the soul and spirit, wherever it is: so is not the Letter.'

Given this freedom of reference, it seems incredible that the details of creation, especially those in the natural world, had so little appeal for those Friends whose wandering lives must have been in close touch with them. John in the Gospels acknowledged his debt to locusts and wild honey, and his cousin Jesus called on flowers and weeds for illustration; but those Quakers so intent on an inward light did not see it shining in singing birds or the wild flowers which were so much more abundant in their day than in our own. The body is more than the raiment, but that raiment is just as sustaining as the spirit can be to the body.

The span of no more than a brief lifetime had passed between the clarion voices of Elizabethan England and the awakening of Fox's revelation. Cross-fertilisation should surely have produced something greater and more lasting than a culture limited to spiritual guidance? The stories so rich in faith and character, clearly shown to us by Braithwaite, could have provided material for many forms of art, but the two neighbouring groups stood apart, having nothing to say to each other. Milton and Dryden, inspirers of the following years, likewise struck their separate chords. Suggestions have been made that the young John Milton may have stood in the crowd at Nayler's punishment, and even have found in Martha Simmonds hints of his conception of Eve and Delilah. Fascinating as these are, they do not link the determined independence of the Friends with anyone's flights of imagination. Nayler's own creative gift was only given full expression when the crucible of suffering had brought it to life.

Considering the fateful part played by Martha from the moment of Nayler's association with London Friends until she was removed to prison after his trial and sentence, readers may well want to ask what is known of the rest of her history. 'It is a woman who has done all this mischief' declared one of the more moderate of Nayler's judges. Yet there appears to have been little reaction to the lightness of the sentence given to the women. The support they gave him during his punishment was such that it inflated his 'crime' while making it more difficult for him to shake them off, had he wished to at that stage.

It should be remembered that the two couples, Simmonds and Strangers, could not be condemned for their extravagances without admitting that they had been respected and trusted by various well-known figures. Only weeks before the trial Major-General Desborough had acknowledged his debt to Martha for her skilled nursing of his wife by freeing the whole party, with Nayler, from Exeter Jail. When Nayler himself had been removed, the disturbances started in his name were increased all over the country, Martha being named as their instigator. There is, as often happens in Quaker chronicles of the period, a sudden silence about her life for the next few years until she is recorded in a letter as having died in 1665 during an unidentified voyage to Maryland, at the age of thirty-nine. One would have liked to know the circumstances of that voyage, and what impact she had planned to make on the settlers there.

Our greatest regret in surveying Nayler's life must be the lack of evidence from his early years. George Fox, enlarging much later on the rough notes he had kept in youth, and with plenty of testimony from others, presented a living picture of his own character with all its outstanding qualities and occasional inconsistencies. In his famous letter 'to Friends in the Ministry', so often quoted, he lays down the conditions required *before* they 'will come to walk cheerfully over the world, answering that of God in every one': they must first 'be a terror to all the adversaries of God, and a dread'. Much evidence of both sides of this prophetic figure can be found in George's *Journal*, and a great deal of the satisfaction with which he described in detail the various sad fates of wrongdoers. Pity for their undoing does not seem to have occurred to him; they deserved it, that was all. He was piling up God's credit without the redemptive spirit of 'I come not to call the righteous, but sinners to repentance'.

What would we have found if James had kept a comparable record, especially of the large slice of his life spent in the army? It would be surprising if he had kept no notes of that time. Dying at forty-two he would never have had the opportunity to hunt them out of his papers at home and transcribe them. We remember that he had a wife, and probably all the details of his service and travels went into letters to her. He began writing books of Quaker witness in the year following his convincement, and increased production every year until his collapse.

It seems that Thomas Simmonds, husband of Martha, who was the principal publisher of Friends' writings, must have played an important part in Nayler's fateful years, and was likely to have introduced James to his wife. Martha belonged to a radical family dangerous in Government eyes. Her brother, Simmonds' co-publisher Giles Calvert, had actively supported the Levellers' campaigns. Simmonds, at first an ardent admirer of Nayler, sent a letter of warning to his wife at Bristol, ending with the cryptic 'Part of the army that fell at Burford was your figure'. Was Cromwell, who was inclined to respect the Quakers, influenced against James when he learned that he had been involved with Martha? As Protector, he had soon found that power had brought with it the necessity to act ruthlessly against opposition (as in Ireland): so he had acted against the Levellers at Burford. Had this uneasy memory caused his silence when he might have been able to intervene in James' case? And on James' side, might not the knowledge of these undercurrents have resulted in his cool reception of Cromwell's last emissary?

James had seen through power of any kind. His search, as he walked away from London in October 1660, was for a country of a different sort: 'Its crown is meekness... It takes its kingdom with entreaty and not with contention, and keeps it by lowliness of mind.' There had always been something of the pilgrim about him, through the exacting phases of his life, and usually he must have been conscious of two sides to his character, the likeable companion, open to friendship and communication, with gifts of speech and witty rejoinders, side by side with a self that lived apart, less confident, lonely and impressionable, a prey for the advances of others. In the final state, 'alone, being forsaken', he had found that this uncertain traveller, kept at bay in his years of success, was his real self. Given freedom it could call on a strength that came to him through simplicity, forgiveness and courage. He knew now that these were not his own, but were available to all through the master who had sown the seed which Friends called the Inward Light.

Looking at the scene from which the early Quakers drew their inspiration, it may not seem far-fetched to compare the two outstanding leaders, Fox and Nayler, with Peter and John. One was the rock on which a church could be built: the other was 'the disciple whom Jesus loved'.

James Nayler: reproduced from an engraving in Klachte der Quakers *... (1657), 'after a painting by Rembrandt c.1644'.*

Index

ALDAM, Thomas
Joins Quakers, 12
APPLEBY, 28-31
ARDSLEY HALL, 2
Reputed residence of JN
AUDLAND, John, 34
Left Bristol with JN, 47
Analysis of JN's case, 67
Earlier work in Bristol, 97

BENSON, Gervase, 30, 31
BILLINGSLEY, John, Vicar of
Chesterfield
Debate with JN, 34
BITTLE, William G, *James Nayler,
the Quaker Indicted by Parliament*,
105
BOLTON, John
Rode with JN from Bristol, 47
Imprisoned with JN at Exeter, 48
At Reconciliation Meeting, 93
BRAILSFORD, M. R., *A Quaker
from Cromwell's Army*, 105
BRAITHWAITE, William C.,
Beginnings of Quakerism, 105
BRISTOL FRIENDS
Reactions to JN and to Martha at
meetings in Bristol, 47
Moderation in favour of JN, 80
'Act of Contrition', 97-9
BULL AND MOUTH, THE, 37,
39, 64, 75
BURROUGH, Edward, 34
At work in London, 37
To Ireland, 39
Return, and interruption of
meetings, 44

At Reconciliation Meeting, 93
Speaker at Chalfont, 96
Early death, 103
BUTTERY, Isabel, 37, 81

CALVERT, Giles, 108
CAMM, John, 34, 97
CATON, William, 34, 93
CHESTERFIELD
Debate with Vicar, 34-5
CROMWELL, Oliver
Creating Army of Ironsides, 5
JN joins New Model Army, 5
Scottish campaign, 7
JN writes to OC, 9
Attack on Levellers, 10
Examines Fox in London, 38
Disillusionment as Protector, 69
Asks for 'grounds and reasons', 77
'Unseen influence', 83
Recommending a Minister for JN,
85
Sends Secretary to visit JN, 88
CROMWELL, Richard
Postpones JN's release, 92

DARCY, Lady Abigail
Attending JN's meetings, 42, 64,
67
DEACON, Rev. John, 3, 58, 59, 61
Accuses JN of immorality, 62
DERBYSHIRE
JN disputes with priests, 35
DESBOROUGH, Major-General
John
Not unsympathetic to Friends, 48
His wife nursed by Martha, 52
Recommends Order of Release, 52

DEWSBURY, William
  Contact with JN in Yorkshire, 11
  Writing to JN in Exeter, 49
  Writing to JN in London, 67
  Working to reconcile JN and GF, 91
  Meeting to reconcile JN and GF, 93-5
  Later imprisonment, 103
DOWNER, Ann, 46
DOWNING, George
  Principal accuser in Parliament, 65
DRING, Robert
  Host to JN in Moorfields, 38
DUNBAR, Battle of (1650)
  Report of JN preaching, 7

EDMUNDSON, William
  Leading Friend in Ireland, 66
ELLWOOD, Thomas
  Meeting JN at Chalfont, 96-7
ERBURY, Dorcas
  'Death' and revival at Exeter Jail, 55
  Testifying at Bristol, 63
  Questioned in London, 65

FAIRFAX, General Sir Thomas
  Commander of Parliamentary Army, 5
FARMER, Rev. Ralph
  Adversary of JN, 61, 62
FARNSWORTH, Richard, 12
  Writes to JN and travels with him 19
  Writes about JN at Exeter, 50
  At Reconciliation Meeting, 93
  Early death, 103
FELL, Margaret
  JN visits at Swarthmoor, 20
  Reaction to reports from Exeter, 52, 53
  Adoration of Friends, 44
  Sends £2 to JN at Appleby, 28
  JN appeals to MF for reconciliation, 90, 92
  Later support of Fox's viewpoint, 104

FELL, Judge Thomas
  Character and reaction to Quakers, 21-22
FIENNES, Celia, 82
FOGELKLOU, Emilia
  The Rebel Saint, 105
FOX, George
  Visits Doncaster and Wakefield, 11
  First meeting with JN, 11
  Protest in Marshall's church, 18
  'Man of the Moment' in London, 39
  To Walney Island, 22-24
  Dubbed 'The Quakers' Pope', 43
  Imprisoned at Launceston, 45-55
  At meeting in Exeter Jail, 55
  Visiting JN in Exeter Jail, 56
  His warning to Bristol Friends, 60
  Riding through England and Wales, 61
  Absent from JN's trial, 66
  Letters of reproach to JN, 53
  Meeting with R. Rich in Bristol, 86
  Reconciliation Meeting, 93
  Later travels, 103

GOUGH, Thomas
  Evidence of JN's oratory, 7

HOLLISTER, Dennis, 61
HOWGILL, Francis
  Imprisoned with JN at Kirkby Stephen, 27
  Imprisoned with JN at Appleby, 28-31
  Work in London, 37
  To Ireland, 39
  Return, and conflict with Simmonds, 44
  Leaving Bristol with JN, 47
  At Reconciliation Meeting, 93
  Early death, 103
HUBBERTHORNE, Richard
  Visiting JN at Exeter, 54-56
  Recording JN's interview at Bridewell, 77-78
  Reporting GF's letter to JN, 99
  Early death, 103

INSTRUMENT OF
GOVERNMENT, 69

KENDAL
JN's encounter with priests, 25-6
KILLAM Brothers
Early followers of Fox, 12
KIRKBY STEPHEN
Night in lock-up with Howgill, 27

LAMBERT, General John
(in command of Northern Forces)
Promotes JN to Quartermaster, 6
Testimony at JN's trial, 70-1
Requests doctors for JN, 76
LAMPITT, Rev. William
Opposition of Fox to, 20
An 8-year-old's Epistle to, 20
LANCASTER, James
Resisting his wife's attack on Fox, 24
LANCASTER SESSIONS, 24, 25
LAUNCESTON
GF in prison, 45-55
Martha's defiance, 53
LAWRENCE, Lord President, 72
LILBURNE, John
And the Levellers, 10, 31, 108

MALYN, William
Sent by Cromwell to visit JN, 88
MARSHALL, Christopher
Minister at Woodchurch, 10, 29
Opposed by Fox, 18
MILTON, John
Did he witness JN's punishment?, 107

NAYLER, Anne
Marriage to JN, 4
His return from war, 9
Her role in JN's absence, 12
Visits JN in Appleby Jail, 29, 30
Character, 36
JN revisiting at home, 39, 40
Reports of trial, 81
Journey to London, 82
Visit to JN in Bridewell, 83
Her Petition to Council, 84
Family's brief re-union, 89
NAYLER, James
Childhood and schooling, 2-3
Marriage and parenthood, 4-5
Portraits, 3
Army service, 5-7
First meeting with Fox, 11
Call to service, and resistance, 15-17
Second meeting with Fox, 16
Leaving home, 17
Excommunicated, 18
First visit to Swarthmoor, 22
Encounter with priests at Kendal, 25-6
Imprisonment and trial at Appleby, 27-33
Arrival in London, 38
Brief visit to Yorkshire and Lincoln, 39
Breakdown and collapse, 44
Travelling to Bristol, 46
Martha's interruption, 47
Arrested on way to Launceston, 48
In Exeter Jail, 51-58
A revival from apparent death, 55
Clashes with Fox at Exeter, 52-56
Entry into Bristol, 59
To White Hart Inn, 61
Questioned by Committee, 62, 63
Return to London, 64
Examined by Parliamentary Committee, 65-72
Support from Robert Rich, 67
The Sentence, 73
Stages of punishment, 75, 78-9
Bristol, 79-80
Reply to Rich's argument, 87
Visited by Cromwell's Secretary, 88
'Sick Leave' to North of England, 88-9
Visit to his family, 89
Return to prison, 90
Sends Declaration to Parliament, 91
Release, and visit to Reading, 92

'Reconciliation' Meeting, 93-5
Letter to Charles II, 95
Letter to Governor Endicott, 96
Meeting with Tom Ellwood and
    Father, 96-7
Visit to Bristol Friends, 97-8
JN in demand for London
    Meetings, 98-99
Walking northward, 100
Last days at Kings Ripton, 101
Burial, 102
'Works' published by Whitehead,
    104
JN and GF contrasted, 109
NELSON, Rev. Richard
Warning letter to JN, 41

OSBORNE, Dorothy, 33

PARKER, Alexander
Three visits to JN in Bridewell, 90
PEARSON, Anthony
Converted by JN at Appleby, 30
Host to JN at Rampshaw Hall, 34
At Committee hearing in London,
    65
At Meeting for Reconciliation, 93
Leaving Friends, 99
POLLARD, Joan
'An Ancient Widow'
Allows ink and paper, 85
Admits visitors, 87, 90
PICKERING, Sir Gilbert, MP, 85

QUAKERS
JN influenced by Fox, 17

RANTERS, 32, 39, 42, 57, 60
RAWLINSON, Thomas
JN's cell-mate at Exeter, 51, 52
RICH, Robert
Defender of JN at Westminster, 67
With JN at Pillory, 75
and at Bristol, 79-80
At Reconciliation Meeting, 94
20 years in Barbados, and return
    to England, 97-8

ROPER, Lieut. and Mrs.
Fox holds meetings at their farm,
    11, 12
JN suspected of adultery with
    Mrs. R., 65, 71

SIMMONDS, Martha
Contact with JN in London, 43
Condemned by Burrough for
    interruption of meetings, 44
Appeal to JN, 45
Action against, by Bristol Friends,
    47
Resolved on a Sign, 49
Accused in Bristol, 62
Imprisoned in London, 65, 71
Confronts Fox at Launceston,
    52-3
At Exeter, 54-57
Later days, 107
SIMMONDS, Thomas, 43, 48, 108
STRANGER, Hannah
Associate of Martha, 49
Defiance of Fox, 53
STRANGER, John, 57, 65
STUBBS, John, 34, 93

TOMLINSON, William
Report of JN's suffering, 73
Report of sentence on JN, 75
TRAVERS, Rebecca
Contacts in London with JN, 42
Washes JN's wounds in Bridewell,
    76
At Reconciliation Meeting, 93

VANE, Sir Harry
Attending JN's meetings, 42, 64,
    67

WALNEY ISLAND
Fox and Nayler visit, 22-24
WALTON, Izaak, 33
WEST, Col. William, 24, 25
WHITEHEAD, George, 45, 88, 90,
    93
WINSTANLEY, Gerrard, 10